WORKING WITH DIFFICULT PEOPLE

AMY COOPER HAKIM
AND MURIEL SOLOMON

A TarcherPerigee Book

tarcherperigee

An imprint of Penguin Random House LLC
375 Hudson Street
New York, New York 10014

First published by Prentice Hall 1990
First revised edition published by Prentice Hall Press, a member of Penguin Putnam Inc., 2002
This second revised edition published by TarcherPerigee, an imprint of
Penguin Random House LLC 2016

Most TarcherPerigee books are available at special quantity discounts for
bulk purchase for sales promotions, premiums, fund-raising, and educational needs.
Special books or book excerpts also can be created to fit specific needs.
For details, write: SpecialMarkets@penguinrandomhouse.com.

The Library of Congress has cataloged the first revised paperback edition as follows:

Solomon, Muriel.
Working with difficult people / Muriel Solomon,—Rev. ed.
p. cm.
Includes index.
ISBN 9780143111870 (pbk.)
1. Conflict management. 2. Interpersonal relations 3. Interpersonal conflict.
I. Title
HD42.S65 2002
650.1'3—dc21   2001036242

Printed in the United States of America
1   3   5   7   9   10   8   6   4   2

Book design by Elke Sigal

WORKING WITH DIFFICULT PEOPLE

*This book is dedicated in memory of
my grandmother and mentor, Muriel Solomon.
May her ageless wisdom always be cherished.*

*This book is also dedicated to Elad, Michael, Adina,
and Arianna Hakim, the joys of my life.*

CONTENTS

PART TWO
Dealing with Pushy or Presumptuous People | 35

PART THREE
Dealing with Deceitful or Underhanded People | 67

CONTENTS

PART FIVE
Dealing with Rude or Abrasive People | 131

PART SIX
Dealing with Egotistical or Self-Centered People | 163

PART SEVEN
Dealing with Procrastinating or Vacillating People | 191

PART EIGHT
Dealing with Rigid or Obstinate People | 227

PART NINE
Dealing with Tight-Lipped or Uncommunicative People | 255

CONTENTS

INTRODUCTION

I am Amy Cooper Hakim, granddaughter of the late Muriel Solomon. I remember helping Mimi (as we affectionately called her) with original edits to this text. Mimi would share scenarios and ask my opinion on the relevance of topics. I recall sitting side by side as we checked and rechecked the index.

Mimi played such an integral role in my life. She taught me many important life lessons and even introduced me to the field of industrial-organizational psychology. On a personal level, Mimi encouraged me to think about my future actions before reacting. She taught me to use patience, logic, and tact when responding to difficult people. And she reminded me that there are always multiple ways to view the same situation.

The most important advice that Mimi gave me was to realize the worth of various people in various places in our lives. *You can have different friends for different purposes,* she would tell me. *Some might be friends you confide in, while others might be friends in a book club.* Through Mimi's gentle yet straightforward guidance, I learned to appreciate people for who they are. Instead of focusing on what is wrong with a person or relationship, recognize what is *right*. And focus energy on the many positives instead of harping on the negatives.

Working with Difficult People expands these exact principles into the work environment. When we take emotion out of difficult workplace situations, we effectively evaluate what we need to do in order to get what we want and need from a particular relationship.

INTRODUCTION

It was such a unique privilege to revise this book to better incorporate modern work-related conflict situations and solutions. The workplace has changed tremendously since Muriel originally wrote *Working with Difficult People*. From cyberbullies to smartphones to multigenerational teams, the global marketplace is drastically different than it was twenty-five years ago. Still, much of the ageless wisdom presented in this text is applicable and needed in today's workplace.

In this revised edition, *Working with Difficult People* is still designed as an instant reference tool. There's a quick sketch of each particular "problem" boss, peer, or worker in the table of contents, with additional help from the index. You can still look up a workable strategy for your desired result as easily as you look up the correct spelling of a word.

Parts 1 through 10 deal with difficult people of ten basic types. Each type is discussed in three separate chapters, because you have different goals when dealing with people you work for, people you work with, and people who work for you. You have to tailor your tactics to the outcome you want. Within each chapter, you'll find the most frequent culprits.

No matter how bright you are, being angry, hurt, or disappointed blocks your good judgment. The purpose of this book is to suggest logical action instead of emotional reaction. In each chapter, exact phrases are provided that you can say to carry out the proven strategy and suggested tactics.

While the focus of this book is on communicating at work, remember that people don't shed their vexing ways when they leave the office. You can also use the book when the description fits an obnoxious neighbor or phony friend or manipulative relative. *Working with Difficult People* offers a practical way to help you turn a bad situation to your advantage.

Amy Cooper Hakim and Muriel Solomon

PART ONE

Dealing with Hostile or Angry People

What do people with personal problems do when they head to work? They stuff their troubles in their briefcase and growl at anyone who gets in their way.

Some are chronic belligerents who take out their anger on you. They are so weighted down by jealousy, rage, or resentment that only by throwing stones at others do they get the lift they need to go on. To overcome their inferiority and anxiety, they act in a superior and aggressive way. They actually *need* to intimidate and deflate you and treat you as a nonperson, in order to bolster their own feeling of self-worth.

Whether you are their boss, colleague, or subordinate, they'll find your vulnerable area and whack you right in your Achilles' heel.

And what do you do when that happens? You get angry, too, and think about how badly you've been treated. As long as you sit there licking your wounds, you're not focusing on how to deal with these belligerents to get the results you want.

CHAPTER 1

WHEN YOUR BOSS IS BELLIGERENT

- **Narcissists**
- **Bullies**
- **Ruthless Monsters**

F irst, let's admit it: We've all pulled idiotic maneuvers, and, frankly, we deserved it when the boss got enraged. Managers correct mistakes. That's their right.

But no one can give a boss the right to call you an ignoramus, especially in front of an audience. Somehow you have to reduce the abuse dished out by narcissistic, bullying, or heartless villains. Telling them off and storming out in a huff won't help. The fleeting satisfaction you receive from landing a verbal punch is a luxury you can't afford.

We're going to look at a better method for letting go of the hurt and going after what's *really* important to you: getting ahead in your job. You'll choose different strategies, depending on whether or not the boss is intentionally hostile. Either way, you can't *assume* you know what bosses want from you; they themselves must tell you what's on their minds.

However, you can't reason with the enraged. Wait until the boss calms down, then talk it over and, at least, agree on objectives. Listen hard, plot your strategy, and think before you speak up. That's how to handle a hostile boss.

NARCISSISTS

Narcissists are ego-driven, big-headed, cold-blooded individuals who expect total loyalty from others without being loyal in return.

Narcissistic bosses take all the credit for any successes at work and lash out at those who do not demonstrate their trustworthiness. They are sneaky because they outwardly appear cool, calm, and collected. Yet those who know them feel that they are ticking time bombs and tiptoe around them so as not to be in their path.

Narcissists have the uncanny ability to make you feel like gold one moment and like dirt the next. When they explode, it's with a no-holds-barred attitude. Anything is fair game, including exposing information that was shared in private.

Of course, your boss *should* expect loyalty. However, not knowing when you will be in the "hot seat" is demoralizing and unnerving.

What You're Thinking

When I took this job, I had no idea that my polished boss could be so mean! I've learned that my day is much more pleasant if I can stay below his radar. Knowing that my actions are constantly being scrutinized has me jumping out of my skin. Just the other day, my boss praised me privately and then outwardly embarrassed me five minutes later because he felt that I crossed him. What's next? Why is he so flippant and hypercritical?

A Narcissist's Thoughts

I'm responsible for this whole team. None of these workers would be anywhere without me. I can be someone's best friend or worst enemy. If people cross the line with me, then they deserve to be exposed and ridiculed. After all, why should I respect workers who aren't loyal to me?

STRATEGY

Your goal is to be treated with respect by reducing hostility and developing mutual trust.

1. *Respect yourself.* You can speak up without either cringing or being insubordinate.
2. *Clarify expectations.* Don't leave a conversation without fully understanding what is expected. Then, create a paper trail by recapping your conversation by email.
3. *Highlight priorities.* Stress what's important to the company—getting assigned work completed and performed well.

TACTICAL TALK

Boss: *(In public.) I need [xyz] done by tomorrow. I'm expecting perfection. You used to be my shining star, but I'm not so sure I can count on you anymore. Maybe I should just give this project to Billy.*

You: *What you are asking me to do now is different from what we discussed yesterday. I sent you an email right after our other conversation, to make sure that we were on the same page.*

Boss: *Do you think I have time to read all the emails that come through my inbox?*

You: *I know that we both have the same goal, which is to do work correctly the first time. I want to meet your standards but am confused about* *expectations. Is it more important for me to change direction now or to meet the original deadline?*

> **Tip:** Narcissists lack self-confidence, which is why they are so quick to turn on you if your actions will make them look bad. Emphasize your loyalty while standing your ground and you'll be back on their good side in no time. Still, always keep one eye open due to their unpredictable nature.

BULLIES

Bullies are habitually cruel, threatening your present and future because loss of control frightens them.

Bullies believe they can maintain control if they use hate and fear as weapons. They appear self-confident and strong because they intimidate weaker people. If you submit, or act afraid, or react with rage, that proves to them that you are inferior and deserve to be disparaged.

When these bosses belittle you, crushing your self-confidence with their authoritarian threats, your best defense is an offense. You have to stand up to the Bully.

What You're Thinking

My boss tortures me with emotional blackmail. If I don't do exactly what she wants when she wants, I'll never get a raise or move up; she could even make me lose my job. I can't afford to upset her, so I hide my anger. But my stomach is in knots over working with this ogre. I'm always tense and on edge.

A Bully's Thoughts

These people make me mad. They're so weak and stupid. They can't think anything through. Well, I told them the right way to handle it. Yes, it *was* the right way. I'll show them who's boss. At any rate, the matter is not negotiable. I must prove I am right. If I frighten them and show them how weak they are, they will see how strong I am.

STRATEGY

Your aim is to protect your job by redeeming your self-esteem, thereby gaining the Bully's respect. Stop accepting the situation. Arm yourself with friendliness and self-confidence and avoid a clash of wills.

1. *Practice confrontation at home.* You want to appear firm, strong, and unemotional—even if you're shaking in your boots. Make a video of this practice run. Review it to perfect your content, tone, and body language.

2. *Let Bullies vent their anger without interrupting them; then focus on their concerns.* In a pleasant tone, pose questions to get them to disclose what's really bugging them. They may be Bullies, but they're human, so don't be surprised if they react positively when you show concern for their feelings.

TACTICAL TALK

Boss: *You are wrong. Shut up and listen and then do as you're told, or else you can empty out your desk and you're history.*

You: *Okay, Boss, I can see you don't agree. Of course, you have the final say, and I'll do my best—everything I possibly can—to carry out your decision. But it would seem that— (Boss interrupts, but you continue, interrupting the interrupter.)*

You: *Excuse me, I'm not through. Give me thirty seconds to finish this point. If [xyz] causes the problem, what would happen if we shifted the . . . ?*

> **Tip:** Bullies lose their power if you don't cower. Deep down, they doubt they deserve your respect. They admire you for speaking with self-assurance and confidence. So when they bombard, don't counterpunch. Win them over with your strong, firm, courteous demeanor.

RUTHLESS MONSTERS

Ruthless Monsters take pleasure in causing you difficulty.

Ruthless Monsters also are hostile, but their joy is in catching you in a mistake and making you squirm. With an "Aha, gotcha!" look, they get their kicks out of attacking you or threatening to fire you, and it's more delightful for them if their reprimand is given in front of your colleagues or customers.

Ruthless Monsters demand blind obedience, but keep changing the rules to fit their whims. They berate you for errors they initiated and then not only deny any responsibility, but also fail to show you a better way.

With no letup, Ruthless Monsters are deliberately mean. You can't disagree with them without making matters worse. You have to find a way to keep them from sapping your spirit and all but eradicating your ego.

What You're Thinking

My boss just isn't happy unless he's degrading his staff. He purposely tries to make me look foolish or inept. I am particularly upset because he asked me to talk frankly with him when I had any problem with my department, but when I did, he used my voluntary information to give me a poor performance review. He humiliates me for mistakes and punishes me for problems! I've started covering up instead of talking to him, because I think he's making me a scapegoat to protect his own position.

A Ruthless Monster's Thoughts

I've got to shake my people out of their complacency. If I embarrass them some more, I can motivate them to work faster. But this is cutting into the time I'd planned to use for developing the new system. I guess I'll have to push a little harder. So what if I have to break a few company regulations in the process? It's coming out ahead of my colleagues and keeping in tight with those upstairs that counts.

STRATEGY

Your immediate goal is to reduce your daily stress on the job. You can move along two tracks simultaneously.

1. *Try a shock treatment.* Stand up for yourself by asking your boss to please sit down, looking him in the eye without blinking, and calmly stating that you wish to be treated with the respect due another human being. Your unexpected action may get him to see you as a person instead of as a punching bag.

2. *Learn what recourse you have in your company.* For instance, many organizations have anonymous hotlines for this very purpose. Your Human Resources professional can explain any grievance procedures. If your boss thinks his behavior may be tagged "unprofessional," he'll want to do something to avoid getting in trouble. He very well may let up a little.

3. *Anonymous feedback may be better.* If you have no grievance procedure, or are uncomfortable speaking with HR, write to the

top boss. Point to high turnover, low morale, or other pervasive problems. Recommend better supervisory training. Propose a formalized system that enables workers to make suggestions to managers positioned above their immediate supervisors.

TACTICAL TALK

Boss: *You stupid fool. Can't you follow the simplest orders? How can I run a division when they give me incompetents like you!*

You: *Yes, Boss, but which order do you want me to follow—the executive order in the manual or the one you are telling me about now? If I made a mistake, tell me. I'm glad to do whatever you think best. But there's no need to call me names.*

> **Tip:** If the torture continues and you're becoming a physical or emotional wreck, consider making a job move sooner rather than later.

There are many varieties of belligerent bosses. When a hostile boss attacks you, bottling up your feelings can make you ill. Learn to stand up for yourself and express your anger in a positive way. That's good for you and your boss. As Eleanor Roosevelt wrote, "Nobody can make you feel inferior without your consent." If the hostility becomes overwhelming and you can't change the climate, keep your sanity by looking for work elsewhere. In that case, don't grieve—leave.

CHAPTER 2

WHEN YOUR COLLEAGUES ARE BELLIGERENT

- **Raging Bulls**
- **Tacklers**
- **Cyberbullies**
- **Enviers**
- **Intimidators**

It's normal to react angrily when a colleague is hostile to you, or is even aggressive without obvious hostility. Now you have a choice. How are you going to use this anger when you have to deal with Raging Bulls, Tacklers, Cyberbullies, Enviers, and Intimidators?

If you do nothing but cry about it, your brain will rust. But if you admit to yourself how you're feeling, you begin to put the anger to work. You start dreaming up ways to dispose of your resentment.

After eliminating the tactics of physically punching aggressors or "accidentally" anointing their heads with hot coffee, free your mind to focus on achieving the objectives that *are* in your best interest.

RAGING BULLS

Raging Bulls erupt unexpectedly, becoming unglued in a violent fit of desk rage.

Colleagues who were always patient and pleasant now fly off the handle. Like kids throwing temper tantrums, they can't seem to control their anger when something doesn't go the way they anticipated.

The problem is escalating. Extended hours and tighter deadlines have increased tension in the office. Workers are overwhelmed by nonstop, accelerated speed. Advances in technology—smartphones, remote access, document sharing—mean they never can really leave their work. It's always a click away, even after they start for home.

Add to the mix noise distractions, interruptions, the stress of worrying about job security, and trying to handle many jobs at the same time to meet new schedules, and bam!—an explosion occurs.

What You're Thinking

Why is Justin so edgy lately? He always looks tired and frustrated. It doesn't take much for him to turn a discussion into an argument and start yelling. If I hadn't ducked this morning, I'd have been hit with the book he threw against the wall. It upset me so much that, instead of getting my work done, I spent the rest of the day worrying about what to do when he gets out of control.

A Raging Bull's Thoughts

I used to enjoy my work. That was when I had some time off. Now there's no satisfaction, no time for anything but work. I don't sleep, worrying if I'll be in the next batch of layoffs unless I can meet the productivity demands. I check my email day and night to make sure I don't miss an important message from the boss. And as if that's not bad enough, I have to put up with my hateful coworkers. I know I have to control my outbursts, but I also have to watch my back.

STRATEGY

Your objective is to defuse the Raging Bull's anger—to calm him down and win his confidence.

1. *Leave immediately if he starts throwing things.* You have to protect yourself. Just say, "We'll discuss this later," and scoot. Your colleague acts childish; you act grown-up.
2. *Interrupt after the Raging Bull winds down.* In a calm and friendly voice, keep repeating his name until he hears you.
3. *Be prepared with practical suggestions to reduce the stress he's feeling.* Don't analyze his behavior; just mention what you've observed. Discuss ways he might alter his job responsibilities or create more enjoyment. Let him know you want to lend support.
4. *Encourage him to develop alliances.* There's less chance he'll think of himself, or be seen, as a victim.
5. *If the behavior continues, speak with your Human Resources professional and/or encourage him to seek professional counseling.*

TACTICAL TALK

You: *Justin, I can see you're having a tough time lately. I went through something like this a while back. If you'd like, I'll tell you what I learned that pulled me through.*

Justin: *I don't think you know how overworked and overwhelmed I feel. I'm sorry for blowing up at you yesterday.*

You: *I do understand, but there are things you can do to regain control. For instance:*

Insist on taking fifteen minutes each day to relax. Otherwise, you can become physically ill. Schedule a set time to close your door and close your eyes; then you can go back to work refreshed.

Use breathing exercises to increase self-control. That helps you focus on the problem and prevents acting on anger.

List job responsibilities you can change. Can you rotate any among the rest of us? Any administrative duties you can delegate? Should you ask the boss to give you more decision-making authority?

Put back excitement with a challenge. Enroll in a free webinar to advance your skills.

Increase your networking and learn what's going on in your area of expertise. Become active on professional networking sites like LinkedIn, and attend professional association meetings.

> **Tip:** Raging Bulls need to be controlled, not only for their own sakes, but also because their actions adversely affect the entire organization. When treated harshly by a colleague, you may sit and stew, pretending to be working or doing so at a much slower rate. Other workers quit to escape desk rage.

TACKLERS

Tacklers attack you personally while arguing an issue.

These colleagues are so determined to score points with the boss that they block whatever you toss out for consideration and tackle you instead of the problem. They twist everything you say so that you become the opponent who has to be brought down and overcome.

When they tackle you, you know you've been hit. They don't hold back with the attack. You feel hurt but are more concerned with the consequences. Your credibility is being kicked around like a football. How can you keep the Tacklers from injuring your career?

What You're Thinking

Olivia can't debate an issue on its merits. It's somehow my fault that I don't go along with her conclusions. After the boss asked me to head the task force, we divided the jobs and all the other members came through. Olivia didn't do the work and then accused me of picking on her when I asked for her assignments. I have to dodge her attacks while Olivia gets away with surfing the Internet instead of working. If she keeps this up, the others could lose confidence in my leadership ability.

A Tackler's Thoughts

If she wasn't so stupid, she'd see that another approach would get the job done a lot faster without putting forth so much effort. She just wants to show me up, but I'll beat her to it. I'll make sure the whole group sees how incompetent she is.

STRATEGY

Your goal is to maintain your professionalism as you carry out your assignments, at the same time minimizing any damage Tacklers can do to your standing.

1. *Continue your game plan.* Don't be sidelined by a groveling match. Instead, question the Tackler to show you are determined to do the job without stooping to her level. Elevate the discussion by

moving the emphasis away from individuals and back to the issue at hand.

2. *Talk to her privately if she continues to tackle you.* Say that you'd like to have a better relationship, and ask how she thinks you might be able to resolve your differences.

3. *Learn where you can—and can't—expect support.* Determine through the grapevine whether the Tackler has company friends in high places. If so, an ongoing feud could hurt your chance to advance. It's not worth the fuss. Concentrate on doing your job and making more friends.

TACTICAL TALK

You: *Olivia, when we divided the work, you said you'd like the research job. If that's a problem, we still have openings in three other areas—*

Olivia: *(Interrupting.) You really have it in for me, don't you? Why are you being so mean to me? You just love to impress everyone with the fact that you're heading this task force and—*

You: *(Interrupting.) Olivia, you've obviously misconstrued my role. Now the three areas in which we need more concentration are 1) . . . , (2) . . . , and (3). . . . Which do you prefer?*

Tip: You're not after 100 percent harmony. You and your Tackler will seldom sing the same tune. You just need to come to some understanding that lets you get on with your work. To arrange a truce, handle the conflict with direct, clear, face-to-face confrontation instead of terse emails or voicemails, which may tend to muddy the water.

CYBERBULLIES

Cyberbullies attack you through electronic means like emails, texts, tweets, or social media.

These colleagues are worse than Tacklers because they hide behind a computer screen or smartphone when attacking you instead of insulting you to your face. When they bully you, the sting remains long after the attack since electronic footprints never fully fade.

Unfortunately, cyberbullying is becoming more prevalent within organizations. An embarrassing email blast may lurk in someone's inbox months later, even after the boss demands that it be deleted. It's more deeply troublesome and inappropriate when a Cyberbully blatantly lies about you on social media for the whole world to see. Unless you put a stop to it and come back strong, this colleague may harm your personal and professional reputation.

What You're Thinking

How can I get Pete to stop posting lies about what I do on the weekend? On Sunday, he happened to show up at the same restaurant where I was dining with a close family friend. He secretly took my picture and posted it on Snapchat and Facebook with a caption about how I was cheating on my husband! I'm not sure if he conveniently ignored my husband, who was at the bar getting drinks, or if he truly didn't see him. Regardless, I had to spend a lot of time and energy on social media trying to repair that damage.

A Cyberbully's Thoughts

I sure get a kick out of seeing Shelby squirm. She thinks she's so smart and better than all of us. Well, I'll just keep posting embarrassing things on Snapchat and Facebook until she gets the hint and hides out in her office.

Your aim is to reduce—and hopefully eliminate—cyberbullying in the workplace.

1. *Join forces with fellow victims.* Vow that none of you will rise to the Cyberbully's bait. Simply be united in declaring your disinterest in the Cyberbully's electronic blackmail. Ban together to refute any false claims made on social media or through the company intranet. Remember that the electronic footprints of those retorts will also never fade.
2. *Spell out the consequences.* Tell the Cyberbully that you know what he's doing and that you are going to report his behavior to the boss, Human Resources, and even the authorities, if necessary.
3. *Keep electronic copies of all the lies and share them, as needed.* Go directly to your boss or HR with this information. Determine whether the police need to be involved. Act quickly and without pause.

Pete: *(In public.) Did everyone see Shelby's hot new date last weekend?*

You: *Pete, I will not tolerate you spreading lies about me at the office or on social media. You may have a bone to pick with me, but it is completely out of line for you to—*

Pete: *(Interrupting.) What, you can't take a little heat?*

You: *I can take a joke, but this is not funny. I've already showed the boss and HR. I'll go to the authorities if you don't leave me alone.*

> **Tip:** Just like with any other kind of bully, when you stand up to a Cyberbully, he will back down. Cyberbullies prey on weak victims. Project yourself as strong, and he will leave you alone. If not, contact the appropriate authorities to promptly make the behavior stop.

ENVIERS

Enviers jealously begrudge you the praise you receive.

These peers are resentful. They want what you have. More than that, they believe they *should have* what you have. Keep in mind that an entire company can't be fooled for long. Most of the time, sooner or later, we all get what's coming to us.

The worst part about envy is that it erodes the spirit and eats up energy that could have been put to better use. But until Enviers can let go of their jealousy and anger over your having what is rightfully theirs, they can become consumed with getting revenge. You may be totally innocent and find yourself the victim of spiteful, childish behavior.

What You're Thinking

I worked night and day for four weeks on that project to make it a success, and everybody's been praising me and telling me what a great job I did. Except for Blake. He's too self-centered to be happy for me. He said "Congratulations," but I can feel his hostility and his envy. I don't know why he seems to consider me an adversary. My instincts tell me to be on guard for a disguised attack.

An Envier's Thoughts

I can't understand why everyone's making such a fuss over him. I could have done it better if only I'd been given that assignment. I don't think it was just luck that landed him that project. I wonder what he did to get it. I'll have to dig up the dirt about him, because I'm sure he told some lies about me, or else I'd have been handed that job. But I'll get even, and he'll never know what hit him.

STRATEGY

Your goal is to protect yourself and, if possible, help your colleague think more positively.

1. *Keep your talks on a high and friendly level.* Don't let Enviers get you into an argument, especially not with others present.
2. *Convey that each person's effort is judged on its own merit.* One's work isn't good because another's is bad, or valuable because another's is not valuable. Each person's work stands as good or bad by itself.
3. *Encourage Enviers.* Help them define their personal goals and develop their own special skills and expertise. This will bolster their sense of self-worth.

TACTICAL TALK

You: *C'mon, Blake, I don't want to argue about that. We can be civil to each other. If you can't talk about this now, let's talk about it later. (Then leave.)*

Or: *Blake, you have a real talent for making training videos. Have you considered asking the boss if you can sign up for that special seminar he was talking about last week?*

> **Tip:** Disarm Enviers with an honest compliment. Just when they're all set to hate you, make them like you. Express admiration for whatever they do well, talk about their interests, and offer helpful suggestions for them to mull over that may not have occurred to them before.

INTIMIDATORS

Intimidators gain support by implying they can hurt or embarrass you.

These hostile colleagues don't come right out and threaten you, but you still hear their warning loud and clear. You know you are in for some form of pain or punishment if you don't go along with whatever they want from you.

An intimidating boss who can fire you has real power over you; an intimidating colleague has *perceived* power. Nevertheless, this too can be a dangerous threat. With every contact, watch for the blinking yellow caution lights.

What You're Thinking

He makes me feel inferior, even though I know I do the job as well as or better than he does. But I've been going along with all his ideas because I'm afraid if I don't, he'll turn the others against me.

An Intimidator's Thoughts

I've got to shut that woman up! Whenever Ava comes up with her bright ideas at staff meetings, the boss is all ears. She's a threat. When Carl leaves next year and the assistant director's job is open, I want to be the natural choice. Until then, I've got to keep Ava from winning over everybody on the team. I'd better squash her before she gets the job I want.

Your goal is to keep control of yourself. Don't allow the Intimidator to push you into doing or not doing anything against your will.

1. *Rehearse retorts at home.* Unharried, you can come up with quick responses you'll make the next time your Intimidator strikes. Remember, you never have to give an instant answer. You can take your time or pick only the part of his remarks that you care to reply to.

2. *Record your practice sessions by taking a video.* Saying the words out loud lets you hear how you come across. Even better, record you and a friend role-playing. Then, review the video and make any needed adjustments to your technique. Focus on your body language in addition to your word choice and tone.

3. *Force yourself to appear poised and calm.* Pretend you are unruffled even if you are momentarily intimidated. You can't do anything about the thoughts the Intimidator has, but you can decide which thoughts you will let yourself dwell on.

4. *Psych yourself.* Put emotional space between the Intimidator's threats and your replies; for example, imagine yourself encased in a protective bubble that won't permit any verbal attacks to penetrate. Until you learn to do this, put as much physical space as you can between yourself and the offender.

5. *Know when to laugh it off.* If you are new on the job and several coworkers are hazing you, ask a friendly colleague if this behavior is par for the course. If it is, though the pranks may be obnoxious,

they're harmless, simply meant as a fraternity initiation to see if you can "pass the test."

TACTICAL TALK

Here are a few quick replies to the Intimidator:

(Laughing it off.) You're not really serious, are you?

(Buying time.) Don't rush me. I'm weighing what you said.

(Being selective.) I don't feel totally comfortable with that.

> **Tip:** Break the cycle—anger begets anger, and retaliation begets retaliation. Concentrate on your desired outcome to reinforce your resolve. You can be firm, forceful, and assertive without sounding mad. Allow yourself to feel friendly and to smile. Ask yourself: What am I afraid of? How can these colleagues hurt me? How can I stand up to them and at the same time convert them to be my friends?

When colleagues act hostile, don't let their anger become contagious and infect your good judgment. Your peers are having a problem with negative feelings—frustration, fear, jealousy, inadequacy, and so on. Perhaps you can find out why. You can say that your colleague seems upset and appears to be annoyed with you. In a calm discussion, if you will both identify potential options, you will both feel better, because the two of you will then be exercising control. Still, for those circumstances where you cannot handle a hostile colleague alone, quickly contact the appropriate resources to get the help that you need.

CHAPTER 3

WHEN YOUR SUBORDINATES ARE BELLIGERENT

- **Ambushers**
- **Hotheads**
- **Revengers**
- **Quitters**

The authority you have over your workers may seem to give you unlimited power; but since your job is to get work done *through* your subordinates, they also wield power over you. For things to run smoothly, you are every bit as dependent on them as they are on you. If you've been acting like a tyrant, remember that your employees have feelings too, just as you do. If they seem aggressive, they may be angry because they think somebody made them feel inferior, inadequate, or insecure.

Even when you *are* sensitive to your subordinates' feelings, a few may become hostile, spreading tension among the rest. Some pick fights among their peers. Some try to sabotage your operation if they think you did them wrong. Some use humor or sarcasm to try to discredit you. And some subordinates, like children, try to get you to referee their fights.

AMBUSHERS

Ambushers attack you under some cover, often disguising their jabs with jokes.

They wait to assail you until they are safely surrounded, for example, by an audience of coworkers in the middle of a meeting. They often don the cloak of a comedian, pretending their jabs are meant as humor. Rather than be regarded as having no sense of humor, everyone else laughs uneasily. Whether you accept the attack and join in the laughter or reject it by snapping back, you'll be degraded in front of your team. That's what Ambushers hope to accomplish.

Unless they tell you, there's no way to know why these subordinates have a negative attitude toward you. It could stem from something as simple as feeling neglected, unappreciated, or unrecognized.

What You're Thinking

That was supposed to be a joke, but I felt the sharp edge of that cutting remark. Why is Liam attacking me in this fashion? Why doesn't he just say what's bothering him? There's more to this than what appears on the surface.

An Ambusher's Thoughts

The boss thinks she's so smart. She claims her master plan is making this division come out on top. But where would she be now if I wasn't such a good budget director? If I jab at her weak fiscal background, I can take her down a few pegs.

STRATEGY

Your objectives are to maintain your leadership stance, restore any damage Ambushers have done to your standing, and prevent future attacks.

DEALING WITH HOSTILE OR ANGRY PEOPLE

1. *Show that you won't stand for being put down.* Calmly and dispassionately indicate that you're glad to discuss any legitimate criticism.

2. *Keep your tone light and your message crystal clear.* Let Ambushers know they can't hide their hostility with humor. Then turn the tables and needle them by asking them to be a little more specific; after that, ask for a little more clarification, please. Reply factually without getting defensive.

3. *Confront Ambushers in private.* Try to get at the root of their hostility. Emphasize your goal of transparency. If they won't tell you, then let them know that *you* know they've been attacking you, and ask them to stop. Look them directly in the eye, and use a friendly but no-nonsense tone.

TACTICAL TALK

You: *Maybe it's my imagination, Liam, but it seems to me that some of your remarks at the meeting this morning were sarcastic. Is there something I've done that's offended you?*

Liam: *Aw, c'mon, Boss, where's your sense of humor?*

You: *Liam, I enjoy a joke as much as anyone else, but insulting remarks aren't funny. I realize you didn't mean to offend me, but you did. I'd appreciate you not doing that anymore. Thank you.*

> **Tip:** Stop the sniping with firmness and good humor. If Ambushers are willing to disclose to you what's really bothering them, you can discuss the problem and probably resolve the matter.

HOTHEADS

Hotheads are scrappers who start arguments among your workers.

When Hotheads can't figure out how to cope with pressure, they can become belligerent. They rebel by provoking quarrels among their colleagues but may not even be angry at them. You may be seeing signs of their frustration because they have had to suppress their hostility. They may actually be angry with you but are afraid to confront you.

Instructing them to stop worrying, or to relax, or that they ought to feel any given way doesn't diminish their hostility. It would help to get them to discuss their anger, but only if they trust you and believe they can talk to you about their feelings without risking their jobs.

What You're Thinking

Harper has a short fuse. She's an excellent worker, if only she could learn to control her temper. Her actions are becoming too disruptive to put up with anymore. If I can't get her to tone down her anger, I'll have to let her go.

A Hothead's Thoughts

They all stop talking when I join them. They obviously don't trust me. Well, who needs teacher's pets? When Isabella takes extra time off, she gets called in for coffee with the boss. When Mason messed up that order, he and the boss went out to lunch to straighten it out. I keep plugging away, doing my work, and nobody notices me. I guess you have to act up before you can get recognized around here.

STRATEGY

Your objective is to keep the anger of a couple of Hotheads from disrupting your whole team. Help them articulate their anger and deal with it constructively so that they can become more productive.

1. *Review your management style.* Be sure you aren't rewarding non-performance. Involve your workers in ways that will achieve your stated goals, and then reward expected performance consistently, across the team. When subordinates feel they are treated unfairly, animosity can result. Establish your rules and periodically check yourself to see that you treat all your workers equitably.

2. *Wait to discuss the problem.* Don't take a stand until your Hothead cools down. Just talk about the anger she's feeling. Then, when she's able to tell you how she thinks she's being exploited, you can shift to discussing solutions.

3. *Work together to resolve the issue.* Ask what she thinks would soothe her injured feelings. Listen carefully, without interrupting. Nod agreement whenever you honestly can. When you disagree, ask more questions.

4. *Refuse to be a referee.* When two squabbling workers each look to you to side with his or her case, decide whether the problem is in the system and is something you can correct. If, for instance, others are putting too much pressure on them, monitor the workflow and route complaints through your desk. If there's a personality clash, insist they function as part of the team. Be firm in stating that you won't tolerate interference with your standards, and warn them that if the disturbances continue, they'll both be gone.

TACTICAL TALK

You: *You're obviously upset.*

Harper: *I'm so mad I could scream!*

You: *Yes, I can see that you're mad.*

Harper: *No one has any regard for my feelings!*

You: *You think we're all insensitive?*

Harper: *I sure do. The only way to get any notice in this company is to goof up. I get my work done early, so I'm loaded down with theirs. It's not fair.*

You: *I can understand your reaction. What do you suggest we do to make the workload more equitable?*

> **Tip:** Sometimes you have to talk tough. If subordinates threaten to quit unless you meet their demands, refuse to take the ultimatum. Tell them you believe they're putting their interests above the company's and you can no longer bank on their loyalty. Usually, however, you can take a soft approach that will protect your Hotheads' self-image and help them deal effectively with their hostility.

REVENGERS

Revengers deeply resent how they believe you mistreated them.

They are soreheads who feel cheated or neglected. Sometimes they misread your comments or mannerisms and mistakenly think you are disappointed in them. Without checking out their perception, they hang on to the grudge.

Sometimes workers who are transferred because of company reorganization are resentful and balk at *any* assignment. True or not, they may feel that you and their new colleagues are belittling them, and this feeling results in an escalating spiral of hostility.

Also, there are workers who become agitated when you suggest a change or a new initiative. Unless you've done careful advanced planning, they not only resist the change but become angry and search for ways to get back at you.

What You're Thinking

I had to turn down Logan's request. I thought I explained my reasons, but he's obviously harboring some grudge against me. I can feel his resentment and hostility, and I sense he's plotting some passive-aggressive revenge. He's probably about to make some deliberate mistake for which I'll have to take the rap. He could cost me my career. Why did the chief make me hire him? I told her I needed a programmer, not an analyst.

A Revenger's Thoughts

I don't know why the boss won't give me a chance to head up the new program. This is the perfect time, while they're reorganizing the department. I've certainly earned the right. The proposal I presented shows a carefully thought-out plan that can't miss. The boss must be waiting for someone with more clout in the company. I may be young, but I'm smarter than half the people here. He thinks I don't know enough of the "right" people. Well, I'll have to show him what can happen when I drop certain pieces of information to the "right" people. He'll be sorry he turned me down.

STRATEGY

Your goal is to get Revengers to behave more cooperatively by teaching them that speaking out honestly, rather than showing resentment, is the way to get what they want.

1. *Clear up misconceptions.* No matter how brilliantly you reason, agitated people can't "hear" you while they are highly emotional. Begin with probing questions to learn what these subordinates are thinking and, if they're feeling revengeful, to find out why. Work

with your subordinates to identify alternative ways to handle touchy situations. Get them to express the likely consequences of each option.

2. *Give honest, more frequent recognition.* Explain how important your workers are to the company and how their individual roles fit into the total picture. Get teammates to help each other. Tell workers how *they benefit* by accomplishing the team's short- and long-term goals. Monitor progress, praising good work while redirecting aggressors.

3. *Express your appreciation immediately.* As soon as the job is done, tell your workers you noticed how much they've improved. Regular, sincere praise goes a long way. When possible, praise in public. (Always criticize in private.)

4. *Plan ahead when changes will disrupt your workers.* Before resentment has a chance to mushroom, take your people into your confidence. Ask them what problems they anticipate and what suggestions they have for handling them.

TACTICAL TALK

You: *Logan, you're usually so animated about your assignments. But you've been awfully quiet this past week, especially when I stop by your desk. Are you annoyed at something I've done? I really wish you'd tell me.*

Logan: *Well, okay, since you asked. Boss, I'm feeling very disappointed that I wasn't allowed to head up the new program.*

You: *I know you were disappointed, but, as I explained to you, we're going to have to hold off on that. It may take another year. In the meantime, you could be of tremendous help to us by . . .*

Logan: *Oh, I didn't realize you had other plans for me.*

> **Tip:** If you let your workers share more in the planning, you'll reduce the panning. When you sense that subordinates are spiteful, be certain they clearly understand what's happening. If Revengers are hostile, don't fire off knee-jerk responses; allow them to release their anger. Now you can both deal with the root cause.

QUITTERS

Quitters are angry employees who jump ship without telling you why.

You can't figure out what's happening. You're paying your talented people more than the competition's going rate, yet they have no sense of loyalty to remain with you. In fact, they appear irritated and anxious to bolt.

A chief reason may be an inflexible leadership style that hasn't changed to embrace concepts like work-life balance or remote working opportunities. Have you been ignoring suggestions that come from the ones doing the work? When workers know their voices aren't heard, some feel hopeless to change what they perceive is wrong. Perhaps your company offers an insufficient benefits package when they're looking for better insurance coverage, flexible scheduling, and the like. Consider making changes *within your control* that don't cost the company money yet provide more balance for your employees.

What You're Thinking

What a bunch of ingrates! After I've spent all that time and money training them, and paying for their continuing education and tuition reimbursement, they up and leave. Don't they have any conscience? Don't they care about all I've done for them? Charlotte is the latest to give me notice without a real reason. I've got to stop this exodus.

A Quitter's Thoughts

What's the use of trying to educate a boss whose thinking is mired in the last century? I have to have a little life outside the office. My type of work doesn't require the old 9-to-5 constant supervision. When I asked if I could work four ten-hour days, he said no. Ditto when I suggested a trial run with telecommuting. He said if he allowed it for me, then other workers would abuse the privilege. This place discourages creativity and productivity. I've got to go.

STRATEGY

Your hoped-for result is to keep your good workers. This means learning the real reasons you're losing people you trained.

1. *Conduct friendly, sincere, nonthreatening exit interviews.* Stop feeling sorry for yourself and put aside your resentment long enough to listen to what's behind the anger. Determine what is more important to these workers than a higher salary. Sometimes, Quitters are more candid when speaking with a Human Resources representative than with their ex-boss.

2. *Decide what you're willing to change.* What can you offer that would be mutually acceptable? If your workers aren't always in the workplace, wouldn't smartphones let you reach them when issues arise? Could you extend privileges to those highly productive workers who have earned your trust? How else could you loosen the reins to empower your employees and treat them as responsible adults?

TACTICAL TALK

You: *Charlotte, I'm really sorry to see you go. Your work has been excellent, and I'll be glad to write a letter of recommendation.*

Charlotte: *(Surprised.) Oh, thank you. That's very nice of you.*

You: *Charlotte, I know you're not leaving because of salary. I doubt that you'll earn more anyplace else. So I hope you can be brutally frank with me. I really need to understand why some workers are quitting.*

Charlotte: *Well, if you honestly want to know, I think it's the relationship between management and employees. We're not respected as responsible, intelligent, and committed workers.*

You: *What do I do that offends you? What could I do to improve that relationship?*

Charlotte: *Let us do our work without hovering over us. Tell us what you want, by when, give us what we need, then empower us to figure out how to do it. We know more about our jobs than anyone else, so when we make a suggestion, don't shrug it off. At least look at it! Let us log in from home sometimes. And trust us that we'll get our work done on time.*

> **Tip:** When you can't tempt with more money, show more trust and respect. Angry, frustrated, and impatient workers may feel their value is ignored. Empower your employees. Negotiate changes that benefit all of you.

You need your subordinates as much as they need you. Learn why they become hostile. Actions don't always reveal true feelings. They may feel trapped, afraid to say why they're angry at you. If the system is at fault, your workers will gladly suggest changes. Clear up misunderstandings by sending the message, "What can we do to make things better?" Act on any practical feedback or suggestion. Let your employees know that you hear them and that you are committed to making changes that will benefit everyone.

PART TWO

Dealing with Pushy or Presumptuous People

They don't mean to be mean, yet they come at you with such force and determination that you feel you're under siege. You may not be the enemy, but you're still being attacked. They bombard you with their beliefs, they steal your thunder, and they assault your sensitivities. Pushy people are resolved to do things their way.

Boss, peer, or worker, they share a common arrogance. Bursting with unwarranted self-importance, they barge in and try to take over while you're left wondering if you should surrender or salute.

These people long to be liked. They need to feel accepted. But they can't seem to express themselves without offending you with their embarrassing gestures, barking commands, and intolerant views. Consequently, they don't have many friends. The more they reach out, the more they're rejected, the pushier they get. They *have* to dominate everyone and every situation. They are so afraid of losing control that being in control becomes their prime objective. Pushy or presumptuous types must run the show and may not realize they've also run over your feelings.

CHAPTER 4

WHEN YOUR BOSS IS ARROGANT

- **Dictators**
- **Fame Claimers**
- **Blockers**
- **Checklist for Offering Unsolicited Ideas and Proposals**

There's a story that President Calvin Coolidge, upon waking from a midday nap, jokingly asked his aide, "Is the country still here?" Some bosses really believe the company can't breathe without their incessant checking and frequent commandeering of your job.

If the plan isn't theirs, it can't be any good. They interfere with your work by constantly bickering about petty points. If they let you proceed, they steal credit for your efforts. These bosses don't intentionally want to hurt you by coming on too strong, but you still feel intimidated.

To continue the relationship, you need to stay alert and plan carefully. When pushy or presumptuous bosses are aggressive and quick, it doesn't mean they're not listening to you. They're probably moving at a fast clip, and you may have to sprint to keep up with them. Also, it's easy to misconstrue as rejection a comment that was meant merely as caution. Instead of jumping to the wrong conclusion, ask the boss if the statement was intended as a final answer. Don't take the boss's arrogance personally. The boss is the one with the problem, but you can both come out ahead.

DICTATORS

Dictators are micromanager bosses who won't let their own managers manage.

They're so scared of losing control that being in control is their main aim. But their refusal to relinquish and delegate power can paralyze operations. Subordinates shut out of the loop are still held accountable. Their thinking isn't considered, and they're not making necessary contacts.

Dictators make every decision and spell out every procedure. Their tight rein chokes innovation and insults their workers' intelligence. Try to argue with them, and you get slapped down or punished with burdensome schedules and workloads. Dictators resent it when you're right, because they think you make them look bad.

What You're Thinking

Maybe my boss *does* know more than I do, but I certainly could figure out how to proceed without her constant input. I resent the power she has over me. I'm intimidated because I'm dependent on her to keep my job. If I follow her commands for this initiative, the project will be a disaster. It's not that I'm being asked to do anything illegal or immoral—just that I believe the boss is wrong. I guess I could quit, but I really don't want to. How can I get her to back off and ease up on me?

A Dictator's Thoughts

I can't allow my people to teeter off course. I must keep insisting that they follow my directives to the letter. Which reminds me, I'd better check on Victoria again. She seemed to be developing something on her own. She keeps arguing with me, but she sees only her piece of the puzzle. She doesn't see the big picture, and her ideas would only mess things up for me.

STRATEGY

Your goal is to have a say in how you do your job and to be given the freedom you need to perform well.

1. *Change your approach.* Prepare what you'll say, guided by your notes of the boss's past responses. You can disagree pleasantly without saying, "You're wrong." Instead of attacking your boss's conclusions, go the it's-in-your-best-interest route. You don't want revenge; you want input and authority.

2. *Appeal to the desire to appear professional.* Coming across well among their own peer group and with higher-ups is important to Dictators. Empathize and temper their insecurity. Help your boss look good, and you'll look good.

3. *Present your best ideas as directly or indirectly coming from your boss.* You and your boss are a team. You're working together. Build up the boss's trust in you by asking for approval when your proposal wasn't part of your delegated responsibility.

4. *Keep your boss informed.* Send regular email updates. When your boss gives you an order, present an outline of what you'll do by when. Loss of control frightens Dictators, so you have to watch every little detail.

TACTICAL TALK

Boss: *Victoria, you just don't understand what we're up against here.*

You: *You're right, Boss, but as you explained to us, you're anxious for our department to show a higher growth rate than the other departments.*

Boss: *Yes, that's so.*

You: *This proposal would help us do that faster, and we'd expend less resources. I just modified your idea a little bit.*

Boss: *No, no. There's too much that could go wrong. I can't afford any half-baked schemes.*

You: *I do understand why you feel you have to check everything carefully in order to accomplish our goal. So here's a precise plan. It shows what I will put in place by the given dates and how often you'll receive reports. They can be more frequent if you prefer. Do I have your okay to proceed?*

Boss: *I have to think about this some more.*

You: *Then I'll check back with you tomorrow. I think you'll be pleased with the results we can get.*

> **Tip:** You must decide your own priorities, such as financial security or career advancement, and what you can do to bring about change. Stop tearing yourself to pieces when you're convinced your boss is headed in the wrong direction. State your case persuasively, then let it go. It's the boss's decision and responsibility. If you're right and your boss messes up, it's the boss who faces the consequences. Be a good soldier and follow orders. Should the atmosphere become so unbearable you can't accept it, then start a job search.

FAME CLAIMERS

Fame Claimers haughtily assume credit for your work.

To them, this isn't stealing. They're just taking what they believe to be rightfully theirs. Sure, you did the work and you're not getting the recognition you deserve; but the boss believes he earned the credit.

Fame Claimers are pumped up with pride they are unwilling to share. Their haughty air of self-importance advertises their belief that they alone are responsible for results because they are totally in control. If you tactfully accuse them of stealing your credit, they'll promise to arrange some recognition for you. Don't hold your breath. People who are so hungry to get credit are usually extremely touchy if you criticize them.

What You're Thinking

My project was a huge success, and my boss is grabbing all the glory. I worked incredibly hard to pull it off. It was my precise planning and coordination that made it click. He hasn't acknowledged any of my contributions—what an ingrate!

A Fame Claimer's Thoughts

I taught him well. I really deserve the accolades on this one. I cleared the path with the other departments so that he'd have the support he needed to get the job done. He did just what I told him, and the result was even better than I expected. Wow! These figures will look great in my report.

STRATEGY

There's more involved here than satisfying your ego. Getting acclaimed as an idea person and a good implementer is important for your career advancement. Your objective is clear: You need to gain recognition for your achievements.

1. *Share the credit and gain a friend.* Be willing to dole out some of the acclaim. Instead of complaining that you didn't get recognition, acknowledge to the boss and everyone else around whatever you can legitimately say the boss taught you. Win the boss over by getting him to think of the two of you as a team.

2. *Share problems and how you're handling them.* Be considerate of the boss's time as you plot ways to become more visible to him on the important matters. You can ask his opinion without seeking his permission.

3. *Document your procedures and accomplishments.* Send progress report emails to your boss and copy anyone else who might possibly benefit from reading them. Creating an electronic "paper" trail has several benefits: Many people become aware of your efforts, you get the credit you deserve, and, in addition, having this record will help you recall your feats during future negotiations.

TACTICAL TALK

You: *(Sharing credit.) Boss, I appreciate how much I've learned from you. That technique you taught me to process the reports faster has helped me cut the project time by a week.*

Or: *(Sharing problems.) Boss, I want to make sure I'm proceeding the way you want. How does this look to you? What do you think about. . .?*

Tip: To convert your boss from stealing your praises to singing his praises, keep telling him how much he's helping you. Your boss needs an extra boost to satisfy his greed and need for recognition, but neither of you could achieve the success alone. Both of you deserve to paste up the gold stars.

BLOCKERS

Blockers advance their ideas and obstruct the ones they don't originate.

If it's their idea, it has enormous potential; if it's someone else's, they slash it to shreds. Blocker bosses are unreasonable in the way they disagree with or oppose what you're suggesting. They don't want to delegate the act of thinking to anyone else in the department. If you dare to suggest an original thought, you'll feel the tag "Troublemaker" being pinned to your back.

You wish your boss would plan with you, not for you. If the procedures to improve the operation are so obvious to you, why doesn't the boss want to hear any of your suggestions? You get the feeling that she resents your interference. She does.

What You're Thinking

I've checked and double-checked my figures. I know this is a fantastic idea. Why can't she see that? Why is she so possessive about keeping the old procedure? Nothing can fly around here unless the boss introduces it.

A Blocker's Thoughts

These pinheads think they know it all. They have no idea how chaotic it was here before I got everything organized. I spent months perfecting that procedure, and now they're trying to undo all my good work.

STRATEGY

Your goal is to get your ideas considered objectively without antagonizing your boss.

1. *Carefully consider your approach.* Remember that perfect timing is as important as the content of your message when trying to persuade a Blocker.
2. *Review the checklist below before making your move.* Take time to reflect on the questions and adjust your technique accordingly.

> **CHECKLIST FOR OFFERING UNSOLICITED IDEAS AND PROPOSALS**

❑ Are you offering suggestions for the boss to consider rather than demanding changes? All you can hope for is that your idea will be considered; it's the boss's role to determine the value of the suggestion.

❑ Do you give the boss a part in the development of your idea? Mention that this is an outgrowth of something he or she said last week, or that the idea came to you this morning when the boss was discussing the need to increase productivity. You get a boss to hear you by claiming to have heard the boss.

❑ Before plunging in, do you ask if the boss has a few minutes to talk with you? If you don't, you may catch your boss at a bad time. If you know you can garner peer support, and if the atmosphere at staff meetings is free and open, throw the question out to the rest of the group.

❑ Before you talk, do you reduce your thoughts to paper? If you ramble, you're wasting your boss's time. Be crystal clear and sharpen the main points to be brought out.

❑ Do you deal with drawbacks as well as benefits? This is especially important when it comes to spending time, money, and other resources. When preparing a proposal, pay close attention to whatever the boss is saying on the subject. Use questions to get your boss to restate a position. Expand your idea with ways to implement the boss's position.

❑ Can you defend your plan if it's torn apart? As the boss is talking, make notes of what you consider to be legitimate objections. When you speak again, first answer the valid criticism, ignore the rest, and then continue with other positive points.

❑ Did you do your homework? Is it possible this fantastic idea of yours was already considered and rejected? Is the regulation you want to change one that was initiated by your boss? Protect yourself. Ask what experience your boss has had with this sort of thing. If he or she started the regulation, ask how conditions have changed and what might be needed now to meet these changes.

❑ Is your plan in sync with the aggressive style in which the boss paints himself? If a favorite saying is, "You have to get them before they get you," beware of suggestions the boss might resent because he should have come up with the idea and didn't.

❑ Do you ask the boss how long it will be before she might have a decision? Leave the door open by learning when to check back.

❑ Do you give a new boss time to size up the operation? Refusing all suggestions from you and your colleagues may be an effort to appear confident when the boss doesn't feel in command. Don't say anything yet. You may no longer have a problem once new bosses get their bearings.

TACTICAL TALK

You: *Boss, is it a good time to chat? Something that you said today really hit home. I think this may be exactly what we need to implement your idea. . . .*

Or: *Boss, I did a thorough Web search and double-checked my figures. I know that we can increase productivity by [x amount] if we . . .*

Tip: Appeal to your boss's ego. She needs to feel like the originator of any new plan. Show her how your idea stems from her initial thinking so she is more likely to listen. Better yet, ask the right questions so that the Blocker feels that you came up with the idea *together*. That's a surefire way to gain buy-in from a Blocker.

When arrogant bosses are all puffed up, you can gradually let the air out of their balloons without their even realizing it. Work with them; don't fight them. As you experience more successes together, the boss will gain more self-confidence and more confidence in you. There will be less need for pompousness or hogging the credit or holding on to out-dated procedures.

CHAPTER 5

WHEN YOUR COLLEAGUES ARE ARROGANT

- **Moochers**
- **Crushers**
- **Knee-Jerkers**
- **Competitors**

These pushy and presumptuous colleagues share with their counterpart bosses a prideful, unearned arrogance. If it didn't affect your work, you could ignore them or avoid them.

But their behavior does interfere, because in some way they are trying to gain a measure of control over you. The friction causes sparks to fly. They dominate group discussions, drowning out better potential solutions. They nag you about improving the way you run your own unit. They create a constant us-against-them tension. When they try to take over the situation, their poor manners embarrass you in front of friends, strangers, and clients.

MOOCHERS

Moochers sponge off you, taking advantage of your good nature and reluctance to speak up.

You don't realize you've been taken until you sense a pattern developing. For instance, they habitually borrow, with no evident intention of repaying. In a restaurant, they run up the tab, knowing that you'll split the bill.

You don't want to confront the Moochers for fear you'll make enemies at work or look like you're pinching pennies. On the other hand, you know you should put a stop to the imposition and you shouldn't be encouraging the Moochers' bad habits.

What You're Thinking

Maybe Brandon thinks I'm loaded because I dress well, when actually I'm a wiz at finding flash sales online. I manage my money carefully, with a set amount for entertainment and eating out. Brandon always runs short before payday and comes to me for lunch money, which he never returns. But how can I refuse? What really gets me is when we go out as a team after work. I order what I can afford; Brandon and a few others go wild on the food and drinks. Then the bill comes and someone splits the total evenly among all of us. I'm penalized for their indulgence when all I had was pasta and salad!

A Moocher's Thoughts

Grace is a kind soul. With all the money she and her husband probably make, she won't miss a few bucks. The company policy is not to divulge anyone's salary, but I'm sure I'm not being paid enough for the work I do. So if I take advantage of a few of my coworkers, it's only because I'm sure they can afford it.

STRATEGY

Your goal is to keep the friendships you've made among your colleagues while still maintaining your own values.

1. *Prepare a gentle refusal.* Combine this by lending a different kind of support. Offer to help Moochers work out a budget they can live with.

2. *Suggest a casual, self-service restaurant.* Then, everyone pays their way, fair and square.

3. *Grab the full-service restaurant check yourself.* Figure out and announce what each person owes. The Moochers will no longer be getting a free ride.

4. *Speak up before everyone orders.* If there are too many of you to request separate checks, proclaim that you're on a budget. You'll be treated with respect rather than disdain. You'll probably also learn that the majority feel the way you do but were too embarrassed to say anything.

TACTICAL TALK

Brandon: *Grace, I'm running a little short. Could you lend me twenty bucks until tomorrow?*

You: *I'm sorry, Brandon, I just don't have any extra money this week. This seems to be an ongoing problem for you. You know, I'm pretty good at math. If you'd like some assistance, I'd be glad to help you figure out how to stretch your salary between paychecks.*

Or: *(At the restaurant.) Look, gang, as much as I love our team dinners, I have to tell you that I have put myself on a strict budget. I can't participate anymore in the usual check-splitting. However, I will volunteer to take the check and then let everyone know what his or her bill comes to. Is that okay with everyone?*

Tip: As long as you are willing to put up with their sponging, Moochers will continue to sop up your money. Their behavior is arrogant and selfish, but they are tough-skinned and the rebuff will roll off their backs.

CRUSHERS

Crushers trample opposition, forcing their views on you.

They are so convinced that their way is the better way that they are bound and determined to push it through, whatever the cost. You're supposed to be playing on the same team, but if you get in their way, you pay the price. They'll try to destroy you. They'll trespass upon your turf with a driving, forceful crush.

Sometimes a poor system enables Crushers to get away with their attempts at encroachment. Perhaps assignments weren't made clear and workers believe prerogatives have been usurped. Or, occasionally you're caught in a bind when, in formulating a project, your boss divides the decision-making authority equally between you and a Crusher. You must learn to stand your ground with a Crusher or you'll be run over.

What You're Thinking

Ever since Brooklyn was appointed chairperson of the athletic tournament our company is sponsoring, she's become so difficult. I wanted to get together with her to kick around some ideas, but she has already decided that she's going to do her job and mine too. I can't allow this because she'll botch up my responsibility and I'll get the blame. On the other hand, it would make me appear weak if I have to ask the boss to run interference.

A Crusher's Thoughts

I'm the tournament director; therefore, I should make the final decision on every aspect of the event. I can't have that communications director handling the publicity. He doesn't understand what I want to achieve. He won't make this a top priority. I've got to get him out of my way.

STRATEGY

Your goal is to carry out your responsibilities, putting out the brush fire before everyone is inflamed.

1. *Tactfully, but assertively, put your foot down when anyone tries to walk all over you.* You can't survive being trampled. Without divulging any emotion, stand up for yourself while showing the Crusher how you can help her get what she really wants.
2. *When the fault is at least partially with the system, point this out to your boss.* Suggest how restructuring might help. When you and a few coworkers each have your own turf but have to work on a joint activity for which the responsibility and authority seem to overlap, suggest that a higher-level administrator direct the project.

TACTICAL TALK

You: *Brooklyn, the boss asked us both to work on this tournament, and I know we both want it to be successful. So let's be clear about what we're doing. As I see it, it's your job as project chairperson to decide what information should be given to the media. Right?*

And it's my job to help you get the messages you want by contacting my media sources and arranging for interviews, Web publicity, and so on. I also have to keep you updated and coordinate with your calendar. Right? Suppose you start filling me in now on how this event . . .

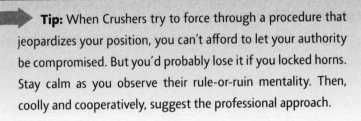

Tip: When Crushers try to force through a procedure that jeopardizes your position, you can't afford to let your authority be compromised. But you'd probably lose it if you locked horns. Stay calm as you observe their rule-or-ruin mentality. Then, coolly and cooperatively, suggest the professional approach.

KNEE-JERKERS

Knee-Jerkers are fanatics who commit themselves without weighing all considerations.

Knee-Jerkers are pushy or presumptuous colleagues who let their intense enthusiasm overcome their reason. They get so excited about an idea, they become full of fervor, passionately extolling its merits. Unfortunately, they spout their vigorous support without knowing exactly what they hope to achieve and, consequently, have no clear sense of direction. Overpowered by their own zeal, they are unrealistically positive because they react without thinking through the consequences. Their certainty that they are right has become such a compelling emotion that it's difficult to bring them back to reality.

What You're Thinking

Anthony is a master at doing all the talking, always sounding off and monopolizing every discussion. He's wasting the team's time and energy. His animated but unreasonable speeches are moving us away from our objectives. But we all sit around like idiots, absorbing what he says, even though we don't agree with him. We've tried subtle digs, but they don't deter him. I doubt if outright insults would silence him. What else can we try?

A Knee-Jerker's Thoughts

The new system I'm proposing would put our department out in front. I bet they'll write us up with a big feature in the e-newsletter, and then that will be picked up by the national news media, and it could go viral. We can be the new leaders in this area, and everyone knows our industry is crying for a better, workable system.

STRATEGY

Your objective is to redirect the Knee-Jerker so that you can get your discussions back on an even keel.

1. *You and your colleagues have to stand up and speak out.* Without being insulting, in a pleasant, nonaggressive manner, take turns at asking Knee-Jerkers to interpret what they're saying and to explain in greater detail what, specifically, would be accomplished.
2. *Press for details such as how their position compares with another's.* Without attacking their opinions, force them to defend their views.
3. *Play devil's advocate.* Offer other suggestions, and encourage your colleagues to do the same.

TACTICAL TALK

(An unrelenting barrage from you and your colleagues.)
Anthony, which companies did you say had a successful experience with it?
What specific kinds of new information were they able to secure?
What were the exact costs of the initial six-month period?
Beside the training delay, what other problems did they run into?
Just playing devil's advocate, but have you ever thought of [abc] . . .

Tip: If you all get together and decide to stop buying what Knee-Jerkers are selling, you'll force them to be better prepared for their next attempt.

COMPETITORS

Competitors must surpass you, making the simplest contest into a rivalry.

Some pushy or presumptuous colleagues take competition beyond its intended purpose. Not only must they win standard organized matches such as sales contests, but they also attempt to turn most other tasks into a clash, purely for the "prize" of coming out ahead.

You can be brainstorming for a solution, everybody offering possibilities, and only Competitors take it as a personal rejection when their ideas aren't accepted. By denying them the applause they seek, you become their enemy.

You aren't aware you're in a contest, while Competitors feel compelled to keep winning at whatever they do with you, regardless of what it costs them. Deep down, they are afraid they don't really excel, and so they feel forced to prove to themselves and to you that they are superior. They are saddled with an unnecessary load—the fear that they may not continue being the best. They're on top of the world when they win, dejected when they don't. All this subjects you to a perpetually tense situation.

What You're Thinking

We should be pooling our ideas to evolve a faster procedure. I like to match wits with Scarlett because she makes me justify my reasoning, but she's making this into some sort of rivalry to make herself shine. She's trying to get me to say I'm wrong because I don't do things her way. She must lie awake at night dreaming up schemes to come out looking better than the rest of us.

A Competitor's Thoughts

Why did I have to embarrass myself like that? If only I'd worked a little longer, I could have devised a winning plan. I know I can outthink them, but they keep putting me down because they won't admit I'm smarter than they are. My coworkers pretend to be my friends, but they are standing in the way of my promotion. I have to try harder to wipe them out.

STRATEGY

Your goal is to help restore a friendly atmosphere, so you can enjoy your work without feeling the hot breath of hostility.

1. *Be professional and gracious.* Give Competitors the respect and recognition they desperately seek. In a professional manner, show them you want to be friends even though they rebuff you. Allow them to feel important so that they won't have to run you down in order to uplift their self-esteem.

2. *Explain the value of synthesizing.* The whole (resulting outcome) is greater than the sum of the parts, because when you share your thinking and extract the best thoughts from each of you, you form a new and more valuable combination.

3. *Be honorable in taking and giving credit.* You want credit for your work, and Competitors should get credit for theirs. Don't allow them to claim as their achievements your efforts or joint efforts. Concentrate on running your own race, not on seeking revenge with dirty tricks or backstabbing.

You: *Gee, that's a good point we haven't considered. I can see where it might be applicable. What if we combined your suggestion with Fred's? Wouldn't we have a stronger force to. . .?*

Or: *I don't mind meeting to debate our differences. . . .*

Or: *Congratulations. Your presentation was spot-on!*

> **Tip:** If your own ego is intact, you can afford to be generous. You can give Competitors the reassurance they need while you are spurred on to greater creativity, matching wits with someone else who's reaching for a better way.

With pushy or presumptuous colleagues, it's not their pride you're trying to puncture, just their influence. You don't have to deflate these types, but you do have to help redirect them if you want to restore a healthy atmosphere at the office.

CHAPTER 6

WHEN YOUR SUBORDINATES ARE ARROGANT

- **Rule Benders**
- **Clansmen**
- **Commandants**

Managing pushy or presumptuous workers—subordinates who are just short of being insubordinate—can be difficult. They may be overeager and don't care how they run roughshod over everyone else. Or they may be looking for something you're not giving them enough of—a chance to voice their thinking on matters that concern their work. Even though it is your right and responsibility to make the decisions, you help strengthen group morale if you ask for their suggestions.

Consider, too, that bold and outspoken workers may be voicing what restrained workers are thinking and don't dare to say. Maybe you need regularly scheduled staff meetings in which all your people are empowered to speak up about vital issues. Maybe you have to relax and give these meetings back to the members of the group.

On the other hand, you may be moving in a fine motivational

direction and still have to deal with individual troublemakers. These are pushy or presumptuous, arrogant people who ignore procedures and precedents and whose aim it is to wield power, either alone or through small cliques.

RULE BENDERS

Rule Benders cut corners, skirting the borders of acceptability.

You don't need a search warrant to find these rebels. They are in plain sight. In their enthusiasm to get something done, these subordinates bend the rules almost to the breaking point or take unauthorized action and make their own rules as they go along. It doesn't matter whose turf they stomp on. They can be equally offensive to bosses and colleagues.

Some of them threaten you, demanding that you change your procedures or they won't produce what you desperately want. You find your morale and self-respect being held hostage as you try to get them to understand the importance of following your directives and getting along with others.

What You're Thinking

I know Carter gets good results, but we've established these regulations for good reasons. If I ignore them for Carter, I'll have problems with the boss as well as the others on my staff. I have to know and approve what Carter is going to do before he takes action, not after the fact. I also can't allow Carter to destroy morale among the other workers. How can I bring him into line?

A Rule Bender's Thoughts

I can't be stifled by their stupid restrictions. If I wait for approval, we'll miss this golden opportunity. And when the boss finds out, what's he going to do—fire me? Heck no, he needs me too much. He'll be jumping for joy with the outcome. I know what has to be done. It's the only way this can work. I'll deal with those stupid restrictions later.

STRATEGY

Your objectives are to get the Rule Benders to obtain permission before they attempt any unauthorized acts and, whenever possible, to maintain the go-getters' enthusiasm and productivity.

1. *Reestablish universal rules and stick to them.* If you play the game with different sets of rules for certain players, you're inviting poor morale, possible sabotage, and even outright mutiny.
2. *Talk face-to-face with Rule Benders.* Emphasize that a) noncompliance is a serious problem for them, spelling out the consequences; b) complying is the responsibility of Rule Benders, getting them to tell you the exact steps they'll take to change their pattern; and c) their behavior is the focus of the discussion—what's acceptable and unacceptable. Praise what they do well, but don't let them off the hook with a claim that their ends justified their means.
3. *Ask Rule Benders to recap your meeting by email.* This electronic paper trail ensures that you are on the same page and promotes accountability.
4. *Follow up with regular feedback.* Be specific with your criticism. Tell them what they are doing right and the steps they need to take to continue to improve. Be transparent in your messaging—no sugarcoating here.

TACTICAL TALK

You: *Carter, I know the deals you've been making have allowed us to expand the operation, but we have a bidding procedure that is* *required by law. If you don't follow it, you face major trouble; specifically . . . How do you intend to proceed so that you can avoid any future problems?*

Carter: *Boss, do you realize where this organization would be today if I hadn't okayed the contracts with—*

You: *That's not the point, Carter. We are discussing your failure to follow a prescribed procedure that could get us all in a lot of trouble. If you continue in this manner, no matter how wonderful your results, we can no longer afford to keep you. I am telling you flatly that your job is in jeopardy. Now, what do you intend to do to keep your job?*

> **Tip:** Be consistent in applying your regulations and in expecting adherence. If procedures need to be modified, change them. If you give Rule Benders special privileges, you can expect other workers to feel there's no use in trying. Any semblance of team spirit will evaporate.

CLANSMEN

Clansmen exert power by banding together in a clique.

These are not workers who simply enjoy each other's company and seem to prefer being part of the same cluster. We're not talking about people who like to sit with each other at meetings or always go to lunch together. Some folks simply enjoy the comfort of being in a group. Let them be. They pose no threat to you.

Clansmen, on the other hand, are workers who flock together to ruffle your feathers and try to subvert the chain of command. They push for what they want (or what the leader of their clique tells them they want), not based on the merit of the issue, but on the power they perceive they can wield. When they believe they can influence or threaten your decisions by the sheer weight of their numbers, the gang is ganging up on you.

What You're Thinking

This group could spell major trouble. They're leaning on me to change my mind, but I'm the one who is held responsible, and I've got to be free to make final decisions. I've got to do something to minimize their influence, but if they sense that I'm trying to break them up, that will only reinforce their resolve. I have to talk to their leader, Chris.

A Clansman's Thoughts

We've got the boss right where we want him. He'll have to go along with what we want now, because he doesn't know how we'll strike back.

STRATEGY

Your goal is to maintain control of your organization. A direct frontal attack will solidify their defense. Your tactics have to be more conciliatory.

1. *Win over the ringleader.* Ask for his help in very specific ways and then be extremely appreciative of such efforts. The more he feels he has your support, the less he needs to plan with his clan.
2. *Strengthen the individual clansmen.* Improve your internal communications. Provide your workers with frequent and rewarding opportunities to speak out, and bolster their individual confidence. Coach those who need help or encouragement.
3. *Dissolve threatening cliques without mentioning it.* Reassign members to unrelated tasks, more suited to individual capabilities and

preferably requiring that the work be done in different locations. Have them report for work and go to lunch at different times, if possible.

4. *Utilize cliques on projects requiring the joint effort of several people who work well together.* This is especially helpful when you have to meet an urgent deadline.

TACTICAL TALK

You: *Chris, I've run into a little problem and I need your help. Could you round up four more people to meet in my office in half an hour? We've just been asked to compile some new stats by the end of the day.*

Or: *Joan, I'm reassigning you to the district office. They need someone with your coordinating skill. . . .*

 Tip: Don't clobber the clique. Utilize it if you can. If not, dissolve it in a quiet, professional manner.

COMMANDANTS

Commandants are very bossy; without authority, they order their peers around.

It's bad enough when these pushy or presumptuous subordinates try to take over your job, but in overstepping their limits, they step on everyone's toes with dictatorial boots. Using their desks as command posts from which to direct operations, Commandants can't be part of the troop; they have to issue the orders.

Although they perform very well, Commandants are offensively impatient with those who move at a slower pace. You've watched their condescending attitude when talking to or about their colleagues. They are aggressive in criticizing their coworkers, putting down their efforts or telling them how they ought to be handling assignments. No wonder negative body language surfaces whenever Commandants' names come up during discussions.

What You're Thinking

What am I going to do about Camila? Her own work is excellent and she's quick—maybe too quick for the rest of us. She's as domineering as a fascist general. Her overbearing ways are antagonizing everyone. I've got to slow her down and teach her some tact before we have a major morale problem. Camila has so much talent we can use, if only I can help her handle her aggression.

A Commandant's Thoughts

I did a fantastic job. Must have set some kind of time record. Boy, did Stan jump when I told him it didn't matter how many people had orders in before me, I needed mine now. I've got places to go and I'm not going to let my dull-witted colleagues hold me up.

STRATEGY

Your objective is to salvage the Commandants' high level of talent, energy, and productivity and yet teach them to get along better with their peers. They have to understand that learning people skills is essential for them to succeed, and that you want to help them.

1. *Give them the recognition they're due.* Publicly acknowledge their good work and privately point out specific ways to improve.

2. *Give these rising stars every chance to shine.* Assign them challenging jobs that look good on résumés. Encourage them to tell you their ideas for special projects they want to develop.

3. *Coach them on how to talk to people so that their words are well received.* Spell out the difference between being insultingly offensive and expressing enthusiasm in a positive way that gets others excited too.

4. *Enlist help from those complaining about a Commandant's behavior.* Suggest they use staff meetings to nail down the group problem of unclear lines of authority. Without anyone pointing a finger directly at the accused, the Commandant, too, will have his say but will definitely feel the group pressure. Your role will be to keep the fight polite.

TACTICAL TALK

You: *Camila, I thought your report was so good, I emailed it to the other division directors to consider. You are very clear on your work objectives, but you need to add another goal if you want to make it to the top: getting the cooperation of your peers and staff. Let's map out a plan and timeline, the way we do for any management objective. I'll check back with you in a few weeks. I'm confident you'll be able to report some important changes.*

Tip: Don't be surprised at how quickly your Commandants become good soldiers. These are bright, eager people who learn fast and are probably overachievers needing a challenge. Once you treat the "people problem" the same way you would set out a business problem (clearly stated, measurable objectives broken down into steps and time frames), they can't wait to exceed their own goals.

Many of the subordinates who are being pushy and presumptuous, infringing on your territory, are trying to get your attention. You can regain control and maintain their good attributes (energy, enthusiasm, efficiency, productivity) while showing them how to go by your rules or be kinder to their coworkers.

If workers are aggressive in volunteering unasked-for proposals, thank them for their interest. You don't want to pass up a potential gold mine when all you have to do is consider the matter and get back to them. If you reject the idea, do so kindly and positively: "Ted, you made some good points, but it's not quite what we need at this time. Maybe you can come up with a way that would decrease our costs. . . ." When Ted finally does hit on a solution to your liking, thank him for being so clever.

PART THREE

Dealing with Deceitful or Underhanded People

These are people you believe deliberately lie, cheat, double-cross, deceive, misrepresent, and mislead you. They use any means to achieve their ends and then justify their underhanded actions to themselves.

Many of them distort the situation. They delude you into making mistakes. They dupe you in areas where you are inexperienced or naive. Deceivers don't necessarily mean to harm you, but their welfare, not yours, is their prime concern.

Some of them put their principles into practice by telling you only half-truths. Their talk is purposely unclear. Or they try to hoodwink, bamboozle, or bluff you. It's persuasion by deception—a coward's way out.

CHAPTER 7

WHEN YOUR BOSS IS DECEPTIVE

- **Hypocrites**
- **Weasels**
- **Backpedalers**
- **Forked Tongues**

Meeting quotas, reducing costs, balancing budgets—whatever the objective to be reached, deceitful bosses move with a one-track mind: Reach the goal, no matter what it takes.

In the process, if your feelings get hurt because they misled you or if you feel angry because they cheated you, it's somehow "your fault." They rationalize that you must have misunderstood them.

That leaves you forced to deal with intentionally foggy directives from gutless supervisors who won't behave responsibly.

HYPOCRITES

Hypocrites are two-faced double-dealers who purposely misrepresent or mislead you.

Hypocrite bosses are sneaky. You can't trust them. They pretend to be your good buddy, but you have to find out from a reporter, seeking your reaction, that the program you direct has been cut out of next year's budget. Or the boss suckers you into creating a detailed report that might earn you a promotion. Once he reads it and realizes how good it is, he replaces your name with his, claiming the work product as his own, so that *he* can get praised by the head executive.

Another favorite tactic of Hypocrites is to take facts and figures out of context or to quote nonexistent studies and authorities. Led astray, you draw incorrect conclusions.

The only thing you can depend on from Hypocrite bosses is that they will actually do the opposite of what they pretend to be doing.

What You're Thinking

I trusted the boss. I can't believe she's out to get me demoted. But she said one thing to me about a new section when we reorganized and then took a diametrically contrary position when she spoke to Mackenzie. And from what I can make of this email, it looks like Mackenzie's version was right. I can draw only one conclusion: The boss is a two-faced hypocrite.

A Hypocrite's Thoughts

Why is Harry acting so upset? He knew we were going to reorganize. I told him that. He made the decision years ago to become a specialist instead of a generalist. That's his problem. I have now reached a conclusion about what should be done with the division. I'm sure I need a generalist to head the new section. I'll make it up to Harry some other way.

STRATEGY

Your goal is to get a straight answer from your boss so that you know where you stand and can plan accordingly. Before you assume that the boss is out to get you, you need to find out what's making her act that way.

1. *Ask questions that require direct answers.* The boss probably doesn't realize that she has wronged you or hurt you. When she spoke to you, it may have sounded definite to you and inconclusive to her. But, as a result, the great expectations she built you up for led to a letdown, and she was indeed insensitive to your feelings. Next time, smile as you ask if that's a definite plan.

2. *Protect yourself in the future.* Don't accept anything your boss tells you at face value until it's confirmed in writing or announced before other people. Once you're convinced the boss has made a definite deal with you, publicize it so that she'll have difficulty backing out. Send an email to your boss that highlights your understanding of what's to occur. Copy others who will be involved in any way.

TACTICAL TALK

You: *Boss, when we talked a couple of weeks ago, I thought it was definite that I'd be heading the new section when the division reorganized. Is that still your plan?*

Boss: *Harry, I thought you understood I was going over all the options. . . .*

You: *Oh, I didn't realize that conversation was just exploratory. Even if I'm not going to head the new section, I've given a lot of thought to it and I have several ideas you might want to consider. (You lost this round. Be gracious and set yourself up to get back in the ring.)*

Or:

Boss: *Harry, I'm developing this new plan, but I want you to keep it secret for now.*

You: *Sure, Boss, but when should I inquire if the plan will move forward?*

> **Tip:** Find some goals on which you agree. The boss you see as a hypocritical snake in the grass may actually be a scaredy-cat who lacks the courage to tell you face-to-face that she's decided on changes because a situation became more difficult than anticipated. You're not the only one who's been victimized by such behavior. Even some presidents of the United States were reputed to be similarly gutless when communicating bad news to subordinates. Understand your boss's flaw and work around it.

WEASELS

Weasels go back on promises they never intended to keep.

While Hypocrite bosses mislead you because they are too cowardly to face you, Weasel bosses mislead you by breaking promises they hadn't planned to keep in the first place. You're left to deal with immature, irresponsible behavior from someone who wields considerable power over your career.

For instance, the boss gives you the assignment you asked for, but he doesn't back up the responsibility with the necessary authority, resources, and other support. He might tell himself that he kept his promise, but he never really wanted you to succeed because, at least subconsciously, he had no intention of giving up any control. In reality, he reneged. He backed out of the deal.

What You're Thinking

The boss has undermined my assignment. He didn't make any sort of announcement or even tell the crew that I was in charge. I had to tell them myself that I was their new supervisor. It would have gone a lot smoother if the boss had backed me up the way he promised. He also said that as long as I kept within the company regulations, I had a clear field to run with my decisions. Then why is he listening to gripes from my staff? He's breaking the chain of command by not referring them back to me. First he breaks his promise to support me, then he knocks the props out from under me. That's a pretty underhanded way to run an organization.

A Weasel's Thoughts

Maybe I made a mistake in assigning Lily. I thought she could handle her staff. Some of her new regulations seem a little off the wall. I guess if I want anything done right, I just have to do it myself. If Lily doesn't shape up, I'm going to have to replace her.

STRATEGY

Your goal is to get the boss to keep his promise and stop blaming you for the impossible situations he creates.

1. *Talk about the problems as his, not yours.* Discuss your mutual goals and what is of most importance to your company, department, and unit. Remind him of the benefits *he* receives if he carries through on what he promised.
2. *Make it easy for the boss to keep his promise.* Assess what is needed and spell it out. Be considerate of your boss's time and make as many of the preliminary arrangements as you can. Send an email recap to create an electronic paper trail and ensure accountability.

TACTICAL TALK

You: *Boss, you told me initially that you had to have a 25 percent increase in the shipment speed within two months if you were going to be* *recognized as an innovative manager. I know we can meet that goal if we add . . .*

Or: *Boss, I've prepared this announcement for your signature. And I've scheduled a motivational meeting with my staff on Monday at 10 AM. They need to hear about the importance of the work directly from you and that you stand behind my decisions. They respect you and must know that we're all working as a team within the chain of command.*

> **Tip:** Tactfully reassure Weasel bosses that you're going to help them get where they want to go. They often have a problem letting go of anything under their control, believing if they themselves were handling it, they could do it better.

BACKPEDALERS

Backpedalers back out of a promise, an offer, or a deal and leave you twisting in the wind.

They differ from Weasels, who never intended to comply. Backpedalers meant well at the time they gave their word. Then something changed, and they felt forced to retract or rescind. They simply never bothered to tell you.

They shrug it off, expecting you to understand. It doesn't matter to them that you were inconvenienced or embarrassed by the unsettling emotional ride, or that they may have caused you to take certain steps you wouldn't have taken if you had known the Backpedaler was going to toss your agreement overboard.

What You're Thinking

He's done it to me again! He told me I'd be taking over when Jamie leaves next month. So I spent days researching and drawing plans and telling everybody about it. I had to learn through the grapevine that Jamie's unit is not included in the boss's proposed budget. He didn't even put up a fight to have it included. I'm so mad. I feel I've been used, treated like an object with no regard for my feelings—not even an explanation for the lack of support. I have no respect for a boss who practices such subterfuge.

A Backpedaler's Thoughts

Too bad about Ethan. I miscalculated when I originally told him about making changes when Jamie leaves. Putting those changes in my proposed budget now would open me up to criticism. I can't stick my neck out like that. Oh, well, Ethan will just have to accept that's the way things are in the real world.

STRATEGY

Your goal is to avoid future emotional turmoil and wasted expenditure of your time and effort.

1. *Try to get a written commitment.* Remember that unless you have an emailed confirmation or a signed official document, you can't count on this Backpedaler to come through. Even then, he'll probably find wiggle room.
2. *Confront the Backpedaler calmly and professionally.* Tactfully explain how you feel and that you expect to be notified of changes in the plan that affect you. If you want to be treated with respect, not as a

pawn to be moved as it pleases him, you have to insist the boss give you this courtesy.

TACTICAL TALK

You: *Boss, I'd like to talk to you about making those changes in Jamie's unit that we discussed a couple of weeks ago.*

Boss: *Oh, yes, Ethan. I've been meaning to get back to you.*

You: *Is it true that you haven't included money for that in your proposed budget?*

Boss: *Well, we ran into a little trouble, a little miscalculation. I'm afraid we can't afford to move ahead on it at this time.*

You: *I see. Well, I have to tell you that I'm disappointed in two ways: first, that the changes won't come about; and second, that I wasn't told of your decision. I'm sure you don't realize how upsetting it is to have to learn from office gossip that something you've been working on has been cut out.*

Boss: *Yes, that was too bad. (No apology, though.)*

You: *I have to know that in the future I can depend on you to notify me right away when you've changed your mind about any of my assignments. Do you agree that I deserve to be treated fairly?*

Boss: *Ah, yes, yes, of course.*

You: *Thanks, Boss, I'm so glad we can agree on that.*

Tip: When you work for Backpedalers, take an I'll-believe-it-when-I-see-it attitude. They don't mean to be mean, but they're not going to let your feelings stand in their way.

FORKED TONGUES

Forked Tongues send you ambiguous, deliberately unclear, mixed messages.

Dealing with Forked Tongues is extremely frustrating because, with these misleading bosses, you feel that you're on a perpetual roller coaster. The boss tells you she likes your work; the next time you do it that way, she tears into you. She says she's not blaming you for some error that occurred, but it's your report she's going over word by word, and she's scowling as she utters the "reassurance." Should you believe the words or the body language?

Another cause for confusion is when the boss is praising your excellent performance and then asks, "Why can't you do this all the time?" Where do you stand with the boss? Which signals should you accept?

While you may be constantly under stress, bosses who speak ambiguously are often surprised to hear they appear to be talking out of both sides of their mouths.

What You're Thinking

I'm never sure what I'm supposed to do because I can't follow my boss's muddied, mixed-up directions. Asking for clarification just results in more of her double-talk. She hedges, never giving a straightforward answer. I really believe she does this purposely. Then when something goes wrong, she can put the blame on me for not following orders.

A Forked Tongue's Thoughts

Why doesn't Chloe perform better? She looked so promising when I hired her. I've tried to motivate her by praising what she does well, but she can't follow the simplest directions without screwing up. I'll have to discuss lack of motivation at her next performance evaluation.

STRATEGY

Your goal is to manage your manager. Clear up muddled messages and open up good two-way communication. Forget the boss's motive and focus on helping yourself.

1. *Act as though the problem is with the system.* Even if you think the whole project is so iffy that the boss is being vague so as not to have to take all the heat, give her the benefit of the doubt. Or, let her play her little games. Either way, you still need to help establish some communication ground rules.
2. *Speak up now.* Bottled frustration eventually explodes in an untimely outburst. Prepare your case and rehearse your talk from key word reminders. Pick a good time for an appointment with your boss to "discuss something important."
3. *Keep your talk friendly and impersonal.* Don't make accusations. Discuss your mutual concern for the company and offer procedural suggestions for the boss's consideration.

TACTICAL TALK

You: *Boss, with our division having trouble meeting this month's quota, I have a few ideas that might help us. (Talk a manager's language. The boss needs to meet the quota. You just declared yourself on her team.)*

Or: *There seems to be a problem with our understanding directions. (No blame or pain from stating an ungarnished fact. Then, skip the cause and jump to the solution.) What would you think about a checklist like this? I've marked points I think are trouble spots, like this one . . . .*

Or: *Could we discuss instructions face-to-face to avoid any incorrect interpretation? You know, sometimes text messages can be interpreted differently by different people. . . .*

> **Tip:** When you think your bosses speak with a Forked Tongue, instead of trying to make them eat their words, feed them some ground rules for improved communication.

You think your boss is being deliberately deceitful and underhanded. Maybe you're right. But chances are bosses don't see any problem with the way they're acting, and you're not going to change their personalities. Again, get back to basics and go after your desired result. First, you have to let go of your anger. Use whatever venting system works for you. Once your head is clear so that you can be in control when you speak up, ask direct and specific questions and make appropriate suggestions. Keep in mind that you can always blame the system for the confusion, which certainly beats blaming the boss.

CHAPTER 8

WHEN YOUR COLLEAGUES ARE DECEPTIVE

- **Brain-Pickers**
- **Backstabbers**
- **Underminers**

Your boss has a certain amount of power over you, as you do over your subordinates, but it's supposed to be different with your peers. You're supposed to be on the same level. You're supposed to pull together as a team and help each other. In the real world, some colleagues only pretend to do this.

These coworkers are so concerned with getting ahead and looking good, they don't want to admit that some of their acts can make you look bad. Sometimes they misinterpret your actions, believing that you're looking down at them, and move to get back at you. Others, knowingly and unknowingly, use your brainpower to generate their copycat proposals.

For the time being, you're stuck with the daily headache of dealing with deceitful colleagues. Your concern is keeping their underhanded behavior from interfering with your career.

BRAIN-PICKERS

Brain-Pickers exploit your ideas, stealing credit for and profiting from them.

Brain-Pickers are phony office friends who pretend to care about you but only care about information they can extract from you. Instead of suggesting that you team up and brainstorm some idea or activity to which you both contribute and claim credit, they probe your mind with delicately worded questions. Then they take your brainchild and adopt it or adapt it as their own.

You thought once you left the street and entered the office you were safe from thieves. But just as pickpockets steal your wallet, Brain-Pickers steal your ideas. Because these con artists don't use guns, you didn't even know you were being robbed.

What You're Thinking

It wasn't just my imagination. Grayson pumped me for information about the best way to organize the program so that we'd have the cooperation of all the agencies under the umbrella. Now I find my ideas in this email from the boss, praising Grayson for coming up with the plan that can help the department achieve better coordination. I can't decide whether to quietly punch Grayson or loudly expose him for the thief that he is. But how can I prove that the ideas were really mine and not Grayson's?

A Brain-Picker's Thoughts

Boy, that was a great email the boss sent out praising me for my coordinating ideas. I'll add this to my list when it's time to hit the boss for a raise.

STRATEGY

Obviously, you won't gain anything from a confrontation. The Brain-Picker has already convinced himself that your ideas came to him as divine inspiration. Learn from your mistake. Your objective now is to separate your concepts into those you want to present as your own proposals and those that need the collective wisdom of a group to be properly developed. Then direct the flow of your ideas.

1. *Plug the leak.* Once you've determined who wants to drain your brain, be polite but tight-lipped. Just stop supplying the information.

2. *Welcome discussion when concepts affect other units.* You don't want to work in a vacuum, not when you need the cooperation of others. But don't limit yourself to a one-Brain-Picker audience. Enlarge the group. Call over other colleagues or bring up these matters at lunch or at staff meetings.

3. *Include the boss by way of email.* After dialogue with a Brain-Picker, share your "collaboration" with the Brain-Picker, while copying the boss. Let the boss know you played a role before the Brain-Picker takes all the credit.

TACTICAL TALK

You: *(Tight-lipped.) Yes, Grayson, that really will be a problem, but I haven't thought it through yet. Why don't you bring it up at the next meeting?*

Or: *(Group discussion.) You know, folks, the boss has requested that we measure the change in . . . I wonder if this approach could work in each of our units. What if we were to. . .?*

> **Tip:** Okay, you were snookered by the Brain-Picker. Be glad this happened to you now. You'll be wiser in the future when you come up with a really brilliant gem. Then you'll know how to nourish, protect, and present your prizewinning idea.

BACKSTABBERS

Backstabbers are nice to your face but very critical of you behind your back.

These colleagues stab you in absentia. They are bad-mouthers, telling lies or being critical about you when you're not there. When you're with them, they act like they're your friends. But out of sight, the phonies betray your trust, revealing some disclosure you confided about your personal life or opposing some action you've taken.

Backstabbers keep trying to outwit you or get some measure of control over you. Maybe they misinterpreted your action. Maybe you did something that angered them, but you can't imagine what it was. You're scratching your head while you're pulling the blade out of your back.

What You're Thinking

I still find it hard to accept that Penelope would say anything bad about me behind my back. But three people heard the same thing, so it must have really happened. I guess in an office you can't have any really close friends because the competition is so fierce. From now on I'll keep details about my private life to myself. But how do I stop Penelope from bad-mouthing me again? And what made her do it in the first place?

A Backstabber's Thoughts

Claire was bragging so much about the progress her staff had made. She's making the rest of us look like a bunch of lazy slackers. I'm really sick and tired of everyone thinking she's perfect and using her work as the standard we should all follow.

STRATEGY

Your objective is to stop the backstabbing. If criticism made about your work is legitimate, that has to be aired and resolved. If not, state what you expect—direct feedback to *you*.

1. *Confront Backstabbers.* Simply report what you heard. Don't start swinging or you'll make the problem worse. Ask them to spell out specifically whatever accusations they allegedly made. Speak up firmly, without showing any anger or voicing any blame.

2. *If the mistake was yours, apologize immediately.* Sometimes you become a victim of Backstabbers if they perceive you were insensitive to their feelings. For instance, if they believe that you meant to put them down by elevating yourself, you could have made them feel insecure, so they want to strike back at you.

3. *Provide a graceful way out.* Smile, but appear firm. If Backstabbers accuse you unjustly and then deny having made the reported statements, let them off the hook. Once they know that you know they've attacked your reputation and you won't sit still for such immature behavior, Backstabbers will back off. But if you create an emotional scene, a tip-off that they got a rise out of you, they may keep it up.

TACTICAL TALK

You: *Penelope, I'd appreciate your clearing up some confusion. I've been told that you said I did . . . Did you make that statement? If so, I'd really like you to explain to me. . . .*

Penelope: *Oh, that's not really what I said. . . .*

You: *Well, I'm glad to hear what was reported to me was an exaggeration and that you didn't intend it as criticism.*

Or:

Penelope: *I really felt offended when you . . .*

You: *Penelope, I had no idea you felt that way. I'm sorry I hurt your feelings. I certainly didn't mean to imply . . .*

> **Tip:** If you allow the backstabbing to persist, it can eventually harm your reputation. Such actions are childish, and it takes your calm, no-nonsense demeanor to make the culprits behave as adults.

UNDERMINERS

Underminers undercut your efforts and set you up to fail.

Undermining colleagues take backstabbing a step further. They weaken your position by clever, crafty means. They lie in wait to make a sneak attack. When the ambush occurs, you are completely surprised. Their maneuver is more serious than the Backstabbers' because it can result in sapping support and enthusiasm and reducing the impact of your efforts.

Sometimes Underminers hurt your work through passive-aggressive means, like purposely being late with needed information or supplying you with flawed data. Or they may agree to go along with a proposal until they sense no support, then back out to leave you holding the bag.

Underminers often level a charge when there's no opportunity for you to defend yourself. When you do, the damage is already done. Maybe they didn't mean to make you fall flat on your face, but they certainly are grandstanding at your expense.

What You're Thinking

Why is Sadie doing this to me? She forwarded a private message that I sent to her about my project to the boss and the rest of the team without my permission. I'm so embarrassed and angry! First, she added her two cents and distorted the facts by giving inaccurate information. Second, she never bothered to check with me before sending this email blast. What's she up to? Why is she undermining me and my project? And what can I do to counteract this?

An Underminer's Thoughts

I'll forward Connor's email to anyone affected by his stupid project. I'll make sure that everyone knows that I don't support this program. I may be able to milk some publicity from it. Then the manager will see how hard I'm working and that I'm right on top of things. I'll be a shoo-in for that promotion now.

STRATEGY

Your Underminer is playing politics and, unfortunately, you are the butt of dirty tricks. You were probably selected as the target because you appeared weak and vulnerable. If you stay still, you're dead and can go nowhere but down or out of the organization. You must launch a counteroffensive.

1. *Prepare a crisp outline of the real facts.* In clear, direct language, explain the facts of the situation. Take all emotion out of your response. If the damage wasn't too serious, emailing the correction to your boss and copying the Underminer and everyone else involved may be sufficient to clear your good name. Act quickly and carefully.

2. *When it's serious, pay a visit to all the people you know with clout.* If you have mentors, this is the time to get help. Share the forwarded message, along with your rebuttal. Ask their advice and get their help. Powerful people who work well behind the scenes generally know the diplomatic language to use that results in correcting

misinformation. Whether or not you have other mentors, go in person to see your boss.

You: *(Your boss is responsible for your work. He must be kept informed.) Boss, there has been some misleading, damaging, and inaccurate information circulating about my project. I've come to ask your help in setting the record straight. Here is the forwarded email and my response. (Be careful not to add fuel to the flames by saying, "If he had bothered to check, he would have known that . . . ") When the facts are checked, it will become apparent that . . .*

Or: *(A sneak has trouble handling face-to-face encounters.) Sadie, I don't know why you sent this information, but it's inaccurate. This paper will give you the facts that you need. I know I can depend on you to correct this immediately.*

> **Tip:** When you have been sandbagged by a colleague, it knocks the wind out of you. Take a few deep breaths, then realize the Underminer's intention wasn't to squash you but to inflate himself. Regardless of motive, you still have to clear the muddied record and prevent future sneak attacks.

Deceptive colleagues use various means to step on you in order to make themselves appear taller. You have to protect yourself, because their pouncing weakens your prospects for career advancement. Responses you can choose to use range from zipping your lips, settling legitimate criticism, confronting your accuser, or launching a counteroffensive.

CHAPTER 9

WHEN YOUR SUBORDINATES ARE DECEPTIVE

- Saboteurs
- Foxes
- Bluffers
- Instigators

With a few exceptions, you believe that you and your workers get along well. You're meeting your deadlines. Morale seems to be good. But there are a few unhappy subordinates who are afraid to, or don't know how to, take a direct approach to resolving their complaints. They resort to underhanded tactics to get what they want. They concoct devious schemes to relieve their boredom, receive due credit, untangle red tape, and pump for information.

These discontented subordinates have a strong need to get your attention, and they meet this need with inappropriate, deceptive behavior. Some try to confuse or outwit you or get away with stalling or faking answers. Others stir up trouble among their peers, either to create a bit of excitement or as an act of revenge or rebellion.

Whatever their reasons for being deceptive, it's giving you a headache. You can get relief by taking a closer look at areas where your methods may be demotivating, if not demoralizing, them.

SABOTEURS

Saboteurs are so upset with you that they resort to inflicting damage in your office.

You tried talking to them without success about improving their attitudes and behavior. Then you find they chose a drastic way to get you to meet their unreasonable demands. Maybe they want more attention. Maybe they want revenge. Regardless, when you refused, they turned to sneaky destruction.

These efforts backfire, of course, because now you know they're unpredictable and can't be trusted: a small harm today and no telling what will happen tomorrow. You can't afford to take the chance. Saboteurs must go. How do you fire people whose emotions are overruling their reason? Very carefully.

What You're Thinking

Ever since I refused to give Maria a raise, she's become emotional, even irrational. I cautioned her that I wouldn't allow her to continue trying to control everyone by issuing demands. Now I discover that she's deliberately messing up the books, erasing information and substituting incorrect amounts. If I fire her, will I be able to find a replacement? I feel cornered because it's important for me, as well as for my patients and staff, to be in a safe and comfortable environment.

A Saboteur's Thoughts

I know I agreed to it when I started here, but I'm doing two jobs—keeping books and being a receptionist. So I deserve a raise. I'll just have to show the doctor how valuable I am to him. If I create trouble by entering the wrong information, he'll need me to straighten it out. Or maybe I can get my raise without his knowing it by skimming a little off the accounts.

STRATEGY

Your aim is to restore calm and order. The only sure way to eliminate tension and discord is to eliminate the Saboteur. Don't clutter your brain with what-ifs. Take immediate action.

1. *Have a polite, professional, and sensitive discussion.* Disclose information this employee may not be aware of. Explain why the demand can't be met. Ask why the request was made. Perhaps there's another way to achieve the aim.

2. *Give warnings and document them.* This can avoid future charges of discrimination and also removes the need for protracted explanations. The conversation should be private to spare the offender humiliation. Send copies of emailed dialogue and hard-copy "evidence" to your Human Resources professional.

3. *Offer the chance to resign.* If you can't prove a criminal act, allowing the employee to resign rather than be fired is face-saving. The result is less animosity.

4. *Practice prevention.* Insist that the Saboteur leave at once. You don't want any more damage done, such as inciting other employees or insulting patients. Doing the dismissal at the end of the workday reduces that risk. Then arrange to change all your locks and any online logins and passwords.

You: *Maria, as we've discussed before, we don't agree to the request that you've made regarding your salary. But more than that, the demands you are making on the rest of the staff are creating a tense atmosphere. I can't let that continue.*

Maria: *Who squealed on me?*

You: *That's not important. What is important to you is how being fired may hurt your future employment. So I am going to let you resign instead.*

Maria: *How will you manage without me?*

You: *I plan to have my accountant set up a new system. Maria, here is your severance check. Please clear out your desk right now. Goodbye and good luck.*

> **Tip:** It's important to control your own emotions and not reveal your anger. Be brief, calm, and considerate to reduce the risk of retaliation.

FOXES

Foxes are sly, cunning wheeler-dealers, out to outsmart you.

You wonder why they're so evasive, shifty, or crafty. Workers you perceive as sly may really be shy, reluctant to ask you for better assignments or for more responsibility. They'd rather be clever than pushy. They may feel left out, ignored, not a part of what's going on. They do what's asked but realize their opinions don't count in a massive, faceless superstructure. Some are ingenious in creating problems for the sole purpose of being praised for their brilliance in solving them.

What You're Thinking

Gavin is clever, his work is great, but I have to wonder if he's resorting to deception. This morning was a good example. How did that contract with the client get so twisted that Gavin had to jump in to straighten it out? He may be trying to outwit me. I'm going to have to have a frank talk with him to find out what he's thinking.

A Fox's Thoughts

Well, I guess I'm not getting anywhere in this organization. The juicy jobs are still going to the old-timers. Good work isn't enough to get noticed. Where can I spark a little calamity so the boss can see for himself how handy I am when it comes to resolving difficulties?

STRATEGY

Foxes are clever. Your goal is to put their quick thinking and shrewdness to work for you, not against you.

1. *Plan more discussion when you give feedback.* Throw them a challenge to find and fill gaps in the process.
2. *Establish a better recognition system.* Give them the credit they've earned. You may need to give more frequent rewards, after each step, or to tie accomplishments to financial incentives or paid time off.
3. *Help workers move out of their one-specialty rut.* Tie training to personal goals and ambitions. Give them time each day to brainstorm and to think creatively. Offer cross-training opportunities, so workers can learn more about different yet related jobs within the company.

4. *Keep your people informed.* Tell them what other departments are doing. Explain how their work fits into the total picture and why their efforts make a difference.

5. *Reinforce positive behavior.* State the problem; explain what the worker has to change in measurable terms; record progress on a spreadsheet; and praise good results.

TACTICAL TALK

You: *How do you feel about the comments I've made about your work?*

Or: *Yes, I see how that causes difficulty. You know, I really depend on you. How do you think you should solve the problem?*

Or: *Taking into account a normal attrition rate, each division is concentrating on reduced turnover. Your project is especially vital to us in achieving this objective. . . .*

Tip: People who try to outsmart you often feel like outsiders. Bridge the gap. They'll stop playing tricks if you invite them in and let them be part of what's going on.

BLUFFERS

Bluffers are misleading fakers. They don't know and won't check it out.

They conceal the truth or lie outright while giving you incomplete or wrong information. They palm off one thing as another, present data as accurate without bothering to verify it, or assure you they've taken care of a matter when they have yet to lift a finger.

It may surprise you that some of these subordinates who lie and cheat are actually obsessive worriers who fear they can't handle the task and keep putting it off. Some Bluffers use stalling tactics because they're afraid if they do what they're supposed to, they'd be trespassing on a co-worker's turf.

Other Bluffers are lazy and irresponsible. A quirk in their personality makes them lie to get out of work. Some, out for revenge, invent "busy" work to delay working on the actual required deliverable.

If you're being plagued by Bluffers, you probably have trouble "hearing" each other.

What You're Thinking

Angel told me the new training workshop was all taken care of, when it wasn't. Now his team is scrambling to adjust their schedules to fit the newly announced times. His staff is having a deadline anxiety attack. Why couldn't he just tell me he was having trouble? We could have made other arrangements.

A Bluffer's Thoughts

My boss forgets I'm a person and feeds me directions as though I'm a robot. He doesn't listen or even care about what I'm saying. How frustrating! I never really understand exactly what he wants me to do. If I guess wrong, I have to fib about having done something until I can get back to it and straighten it out.

STRATEGY

Your goal is to have everyone on the same page.

1. *Clarify instructions.* You can eliminate a lot of the bluffing and stalling by asking workers to restate assignments in their own

words, to be sure they understand. Have them send this to you by email, so that you have a paper trail. Talk about concerns they may have. Shorten reporting periods with *segmented* deadlines. Assure Bluffers who are also perfectionists that they'll have time later to polish their masterpieces.

2. *Devise a better feedback plan.* Feedback should be more frequent, more specific, more helpful, and less threatening. With those you regard as irresponsible, keep the tone constructive instead of critical by concentrating on consequences rather than on threats.

3. *Link individual performance to team morale.* Act as though they've already developed a potential capability you've detected. Talk in terms of the value of their work to the whole team.

TACTICAL TALK

You: *Why do you think you were unable to do what you promised?. . . What do you suggest we do about that?*

Or: *What do you think would happen to our department if everyone acted like that? Do you know what will happen if you continue to. . .? What steps will you take to correct this?*

Or: *Your quick action was really helpful to our team. But why do you think we found ourselves in that crisis? How can we prevent a repetition?*

Tip: Subordinates bluff for many reasons. More direct, face-to-face communication will help allay their fears, make them believe you're on their side, and encourage them to accept responsibility for their own actions.

INSTIGATORS

Instigators are troublemakers. They stir up your workers and provoke action.

These subordinates say nasty things, twisting the truth to goad other workers, creating unnecessary problems. While they don't steal equipment or supplies, they are guilty of stealing your time. You have to keep putting out the brush fires their prodding has initiated.

Some troublemakers are bored, unchallenged, underutilized high-achievers. It could be a mismatch of job and worker. Or, they see no reason to work on assignments they find unexciting and unimportant when they know they're capable of doing a lot more.

Some Instigators are expressing their resentment of your management style. If you keep stressing what they do wrong, they may be pleading for personal growth opportunities. Or they may want to get back at you for chewing them out, throwing cold water on their ideas, or making it impossible for them to penetrate a tight circle of select employees. Also, they might be having personal problems and be taking out their hostility on you.

Other Instigators rebel against the red tape that stifles any initiative. Some have been disillusioned by phoniness and resent compromises that occur in the workplace. They've been hurt and want to expose acts they consider unfair or unethical, because they still care deeply about integrity.

What You're Thinking

Nora reminds me of the kid in school who's always giving the teacher a hard time. She's too bright to stay with the group, gets bored, and gets into trouble. I certainly give her enough attention and recognition. I need to channel her energy into a new challenge.

An Instigator's Thoughts

This organization is so bogged down in overlapping rules and policies that nobody can breathe. It starts from the day you get hired and go through that painful new-hire orientation. I suggested ways to improve it to the boss, but he didn't pay any attention. What if I goad our group into pressuring the boss to change a lot of their ridiculous procedures? Even if we don't get them changed, I can stir up some action and at least add a little excitement to the daily grind.

STRATEGY

Your goal is to turn troublemakers around and help reshape their destructive efforts into productive ones.

1. *Add excitement to reduce the mischief.* Change jobs if workers are mismatched with their jobs, to inflate, rather than crush, the ego. When feasible, rotate jobs for the joy and value of learning something new. Start healthy competition among your team with meaningful prizes. Discover the one thing a low-achiever desires (everyone wants something), and encourage the person to go after it.

2. *Offer empathy to show your understanding.* Let workers know you feel some affinity for their position because you were once in their shoes. Explore without trying to trap. Suggest training courses that could help them achieve personal goals. Enlarge the circle of people you listen to. Show your confidence in them by planning meetings, workshops, and informal sessions to garner their ideas.

3. *Give them latitude with limits.* Empower your employees by giving them the freedom to make certain decisions on their own. Explain why the company is moving in a given direction, then give them a

chance to buy into your ideas. Let rebels become creative by designing a plan and implementing it once it has your approval. Share, delegate, and eliminate excessive micromanagement.

TACTICAL TALK

You: *Nora, I can see you're a natural leader and this job doesn't allow you to develop your leadership skills. I'm moving you to Human Resources, and I'm counting on you to inspire the new employees.*

Or: *Nora, I know how you feel, because I had to work my way up, too. Let's talk about your future and how you can progress. Where would you like to be two years from now?*

> **Tip:** Instigators are causing you trouble because they feel bored, bitter, or restricted. Review your rules, policies, and procedures to add excitement, understanding, and opportunity. Especially eliminate the extraneous to make room for the spontaneous.

When employees' actions are deceptive and underhanded, instead of trying to psychoanalyze their behavior, focus on the results you want to achieve and move them in that direction. Some studies show that boredom is the top complaint among workers. If that's true in your arena, it's up to you to help your subordinates understand their value and the importance of their work. Underutilizing subordinates with great potential is like having money in the bank, except that their interest won't grow if you save them. Give bored workers the chance and the challenge to develop and contribute.

PART FOUR

Dealing with Shrewd or Manipulative People

When we try to influence others, we call it persuasion. When other people try to influence us, we call it manipulation. To some extent, we're all bent on trying to grab control to get what we want, but the shrewd or manipulative bosses, colleagues, and subordinates we're discussing here go beyond the normal attempt at convincing.

These people have no respect for a differing point of view. Because of their need to keep the upper hand, they can't enjoy competition. They don't stop to think how they're affecting you. They simply don't care because they're consumed with achieving a goal—no matter the means. To them, people are pawns, objects to be pushed around and promised anything. They are imposers who praise and promote, taking advantage of your good nature.

In order to gain control, manipulators habitually hide their true feelings. Suffering from a shortage of scruples or sensitivity, they are free to infringe and encroach on your time and talent. Their keen insight enables them to make quick decisions in touchy situations, swerving past roadblocks with roundabout routes. They can't risk being forthright, so their body language becomes particularly important for you to observe. It may take a while to register that you are being victimized by clever exploiters.

CHAPTER 10

WHEN YOUR BOSS IS EXPLOITIVE

- **Slave Drivers**
- **Connivers**
- **Camouflagers**
- **Flatterers**

Sometimes you may wonder how certain bosses are able to advance as far as they have within the organization. You know that you're faster with the facts and figures. Maybe so, but they are probably at the head of the class in office politics.

Perhaps they're slick about avoiding blame and quick about grabbing applause, especially for work done by peers or subordinates. They may spend most of their time making friends and making deals, promising anything and everything. They can be charming in the way they pump you up in preparation for dumping on you projects no one else wants. Or, they may be insensitive when they ask you to put in an unreasonable amount of time or effort.

Whatever the particular manner may be, you're convinced that these exploitive bosses are using you. It is imperative that you quickly regain personal control and balance.

SLAVE DRIVERS

Slave Drivers are overly ambitious bosses who overload you, demanding unreasonable overtime or enforcing a faster pace than necessary.

Sometimes you play right into the hand of a manipulative taskmaster, for instance, when you know the overload stems from the boss's lack of structure or refusal to hire a replacement and you give tacit approval. You let a boss string you along and never say "Whoa," or you never suggest what you are willing and unwilling to keep doing.

You'd like more time for your personal life, but you don't know how to ask for it—not when this Slave Driver insists that you always respond to phone calls and text messages, even after hours or on the weekend. What can you do and say that won't jeopardize your job or career advancement?

What You're Thinking

This is really too much. Since Kennedy took maternity leave, I've been doing her work plus mine for two months. Now, tonight, just when I'm ready to leave for a planned evening with my family, the boss dumps a can't-wait problem on my desk. I can't leave when there's a matter to resolve, but I'm not being compensated for my overtime. However, the money isn't as important as my time. How can I integrate and balance my professional and personal life?

A Slave Driver's Thoughts

I know I promised we'd hire a temp while Kennedy is on leave, but Peyton seems to be tackling both jobs quite well without much complaint. Being lean and mean is really saving the company a significant sum. Peyton wasn't too happy to be working late again tonight. She may sulk a bit, but I can depend on her to do what I want done.

STRATEGY

Your goal is twofold: to gain some balance and to devise a plan that would reduce your hours without hurting your career.

1. *Negotiate for a reasonable workload.* Ask your boss to prioritize your present duties and reassign to others your less important ones. Matter-of-factly discuss the overwhelming pace, explaining that more time off is more important to you than overtime pay. (If more money were your goal, you'd ask how you could be compensated for your additional responsibilities.)

2. *Suggest a way to any manager's heart—show how to cut costs.* It's cheaper for companies to grant flexible benefits than to pay overtime. This also works in the employee's favor. In organizations compatible with working remotely, reduced workweek, and flextime, workers report satisfaction with their career change, even if they didn't climb as fast as full-timers.

3. *Make the case for a trial run.* Ask for the chance to show that you can produce the same amount of work in four days at the office that you just agreed to do in a week (or by working at home, how everything can be accomplished by working remotely). Plan for regular feedback on your job performance.

4. *Allay the fear that you're not there when needed.* With today's technology, you and the office can be in contact instantly. If there's a serious problem on your day off, you're willing to hold a videoconference or to come in.

5. *Get your agreement in writing.* This will help avoid misunderstandings or reneging on a promise. Offer to draft an email recap of your agreement. Copy any relevant party on the message.

TACTICAL TALK

You: *Boss, I enjoy working for this company, and I'm always ready for more responsibilities. With Kennedy gone, here's a list of what I'm presently handling. Would you please prioritize these duties for me?*

Boss: *Sure.*

You: *You know I want to be helpful. So the best way to meet your goals, if we're not going to hire a temp, is to give some of my less important activities to others or put them on hold. Frankly, I can't keep going at the present pace, but I'm not asking for overtime for my extra hours. What I do need is more time off.*

Boss: *I don't see how that's possible.*

You: *I have a way to make it work. I want to come in to the office four longer days a week instead of five. I'm positive I can get all your priorities accomplished, and we can meet regularly to make sure I stay on track. I do the same work but spend fewer days here. It doesn't cost you anything to give it a try. If it doesn't work out after a month, I'll resume my former schedule; if it does, we both benefit.*

Boss: *But that won't do. I need you to be here when a problem comes up.*

You: *Look, I've got a smartphone and I can log in remotely. You can be in instant contact with me if there's a serious problem. And even if it's my day off, if you really need me, I'm willing to be flexible. Now, how should we handle this? Do you want to confirm our agreement by email?*

> **Tip:** Negotiate to reshuffle your responsibilities. Slave Driver bosses are more interested in getting the work done when and how they want it than in making you miserable. Speak up and show them how they can benefit.

CONNIVERS

Connivers imply consent and blame you when the wrongful act backfires.

The bottom line is that conniving bosses won't gamble on their own ability. Taking a risk means accepting a situation as beyond your control, and manipulators *have* to feel in control. Connivers maintain command by hiding behind a powerful position.

They want everyone to believe they had no knowledge of what went wrong. They're usually careful not to leave telltale fingerprints or clues that could point back to them. Although you and the boss discussed the proposed action before proceeding, rather than share any responsibility for the fiasco, your boss leaves you out on a limb. If it's necessary to save their own hides, Connivers even saw off the branch. Either way, you become a victim.

What You're Thinking

A few months ago the boss said we had to seek additional funding. I checked the crucial points with the boss while preparing one of the proposals to a potential source. Unfortunately, the proposal was rejected. All of a sudden, it became "Keith's proposal," as though the boss had nothing whatsoever to do with it. He played a big part in calling the shots and, of course, he had to sign off on the application. I may have picked up a reputation as a loser. I sure hate taking the rap, but how can I cross the boss?

A Conniver's Thoughts

It's a shame that proposal Keith prepared didn't get funded. I thought it had a pretty good chance. But at least the one Carole wrote did come through. So, as far as the big boss is concerned, my department and I are still looking good.

STRATEGY

Your goal is to stop feeling victimized. Keep in mind that if your boss acts the same with the rest of the staff, his troublesome behavior is not directed at you exclusively. Your aim is to secure support instead of being the boss's shield.

1. *Appeal to the sense of fairness.* Your boss hasn't been losing any sleep thinking about you or how you are affected. He's worried about protecting himself. Utilize questions to reveal to him the true situation, questions that penetrate to the core of the problem. If the discussion is not going the way you want, change the direction by asking more questions.

2. *Make suggestions that will strengthen the boss's position.* It's obviously very important to him that he be well regarded by his peers and superiors. Try harder to dig up information, refine it for his immediate use, and offer it tactfully. Help the boss become what he'd like everyone to believe he already is.

TACTICAL TALK

You: *Boss, I've always regarded you as a fair-minded person, so I don't think you realize the position I'm in. Did you mean to imply that I* *alone was responsible for the rejected proposal? I feel like I was left twisting in the wind. That wasn't what you intended, was it?*

Or: *Boss, analyzing these reported events, there's a definite pattern emerging that you might want to act on before everyone else jumps on the bandwagon. Even if we don't reach the projected amounts, your approach will be recognized as innovative and will help move the organization in a good direction.*

Tip: While driving you up the wall, Conniver bosses are similar to backseat drivers who refuse to take the wheel. Because they can't tolerate being regarded as inept, they protect their self-image, probably unaware that they habitually blame others for making a wrong turn. Point out the benefits as you gently steer them toward accepting a challenge.

CAMOUFLAGERS

Camouflagers have hidden agendas, telling half-truths and omitting necessary facts.

Whereas Connivers hide so that no one will think they're ineffective, Camouflagers hide so that no one will learn their true personal goals. These bosses won't level with you, always masking the real reason for their request. They are pleasant and nonthreatening, pretending they are as concerned about you as they are about getting the job done. They make deals: "If you do this for me, I'll do that for you."

Camouflagers constantly maneuver and manipulate. They're so busy trading favors that they're barely able to make their deadlines. And they really believe they can outthink you. How could you learn that what they're suggesting wasn't meant to help you but to bail themselves out of some self-inflicted difficulty? You do as they ask, and find yourself repeatedly disappointed and frustrated.

What You're Thinking

I don't understand the boss. Why did he have to wait until the last minute to worry about that report that's due tomorrow? He said if I burn the midnight oil and finish it by 10 AM, he'll remember my cooperation next time raises are being considered. He forgot that's what he promised me six months ago. Budget time came and went, along with another broken promise. Then when I tried to ask him about it, he was suddenly too busy to talk to me. I wonder how I can ever trust him again.

A Camouflager's Thoughts

Boy, I really slipped up on that quarterly report, and it's due at tomorrow's 11 AM meeting. I've got to talk Natalie into doing it for me and getting it done tonight. I could tell her that I'll mention her name to the board, and then I'll dangle a possible raise. That should do it.

STRATEGY

To the guideline of doing whatever the boss asks as long as it's not illegal, immoral, or unethical, add another qualification—unreasonable. When you can't do what is requested, your goal is to escape without incurring the boss's wrath or vengeance.

1. *Forget long-range deals and broken promises.* The leopard won't change his spots. Any agreement on advancement that you reach with the Camouflager has to be in writing and preferably witnessed. Don't do what he asks because you expect the promised

prize. Do it, if you can, because you want to be regarded as a reasonable, cooperative, and dependable worker.

2. *Manage your manager.* Suggest an alternative to your doing the task. Maybe a rush job can be divided among a few of you, or perhaps there's a way to get an extension. Maybe by teaching someone else to do a technical task, you could be unchained from your desk.

3. *Sound like a team player even though you're not playing the boss's game.* Don't get angry or threaten or remind the boss that you've heard that song before. Play it cool, cheerful, and helpful. A pro pitches in without making deals whether acting as a doer, mobilizer, or encourager.

TACTICAL TALK

You: (*Accepting.*) *Boss, I'd be glad to work all night on the report because I know how important it is to our division. We can discuss recognition and raises later. That's not why I'm doing this. But I will need a little help with my routine tasks tomorrow. Do you think Chuck could take over a few of them for me?*

Or: (*Rejecting or hedging.*) *Boss, I'd be glad to work all night on the report because I know how important it is to our division. But we're running too great a risk that I may not be able to finish it on time for your meeting. How about dividing the four segments among Chuck, Juan, Marlene, and me?*

> **Tip:** Act professionally even when your boss seems to have forgotten how. If your boss is a wheeler-dealer, that's his problem, not yours. You can be above the shenanigans by changing the scenario. Also, it would help you to find a mentor other than your boss.

FLATTERERS

Flatterers insincerely give you excessive praise in order to use you.

These bosses believe if they constantly say things designed to please you, greatly exaggerating reality, they are pouring on personal charm and charisma. ("This project would have been an absolute disaster without you.") They want you to like them on a personal level in order to win your support and loyalty.

They're afraid their plan, procedure, policy, or assignment can't stand on its own merit. So they employ unwarranted praise to gain your acceptance of them and their request *as one package.* Inflating your ego and promising rewards of success to make you want to join in does work for a while. There's nothing we enjoy more than hearing the boss give praise we honestly believe we earned. Conversely, nothing makes us more suspicious than a boss heaping elaborate compliments we regard as undeserved and phony.

This method of motivating their workers can boomerang for Flatterers when their plans can't stand up and you begin to lose faith in the leader you're following.

What You're Thinking

What's going on? The boss tells me everything I do is great. The results of the last meeting were great, but the previous ones were nothing to brag about because I didn't have time to make them better. Does she know the difference between mediocre and quality, and would she know how to give excellent work widespread distribution? Or does she have some ulterior motive, buttering me up with lavish praise to get me to do something I might otherwise object to?

A Flatterer's Thoughts

You can't show too much attention too often to win over your employees. Nothing gets them to strive for excellence every time like compliments. Besides, after you compliment them, it's easier to tell them something they won't want to hear. They're going to have to put in a lot of extra hours to get our department the extra support we need. I must make all of them team players, totally loyal to me.

STRATEGY

Your goal is to get ahead, preferably with your boss's help, but without buying into a phony plan. The harm caused by Flatterer bosses is that they leave you disillusioned, because you sense a leadership vacuum. However, this may be your opportunity. You may be able to fill at least some of the void.

1. *Maintain your objectivity.* Take the flattering remarks with a grain of salt. If you're being praised for a task that fell short, be gracious and appreciative, and then speak up on what is needed for improvement. If your relationship is cordial enough, make a joke out of the flattery and tease the Flatterer.

2. *Get clear statements of desired results and individual roles.* Research useful data the boss can employ in deciding policy. Encourage group discussions from which better strategies and clear blueprints can emerge. A team that has a part in the planning is automatically more interested in the outcome. You can raise the morale of your group without being the boss.

You: *I appreciate the kind remarks, Boss, but I know you'd like it to be even better. It seems to me that if we could allot a little more staff time and equipment, we could more than double . . .*

Or: *Okay, Boss, this flattery will get you whatever you want.*

Or: *Don't you think we need a tighter plan to make this succeed? It seems to me we have to break down the stages into . . .*

> **Tip:** A Flatterer boss gives you the chance to enhance your own leadership skills. Help your boss plan to stand on firmer ground so that he won't have to rely on phony compliments to motivate the team.

Some bosses deliberately drain every last ounce of work out of you, or cover up their real reasons for their requests, or blame you in order to protect themselves. More often, exploitive bosses act like that because they are preoccupied or insensitive, unaware that they appear to be tricky. You're ensnared only when you're too scared to speak up. There are always other options to suggest. You can be cooperative without becoming the fly who steps into the spider's web.

CHAPTER 11

WHEN YOUR COLLEAGUES
ARE EXPLOITIVE

- **Imposers**
- **Duck and Divers**
- **Operators**

Many colleagues who take advantage of you don't intentionally try to hurt you. More likely, they've put their personal feelings about you aside as they analyze what is needed to accomplish their goals. To them, how they feel about you is quite beside the point.

This absence of emotion, which you perceive as deceitful, rude, or insensitive, allows them to use you to get what they're after. They play their hands with finesse, knowing how you will most probably react, and planning their countermoves ahead if you should present an obstacle.

When you feel that you're being tricked or exploited, you'd like to give in to your rage and attack the manipulators. However, all that does is show everyone else that you've lost control.

You have to stop dead in your tracks until you figure out what your colleague is trying to get away with. Only then can you respond accordingly, in a logical and positive fashion.

IMPOSERS

Imposers take unfair advantage of your time, talent, and good nature.

Colleagues such as these are just plain self-centered and inconsiderate of others. You certainly don't mind doing a favor every once in a while, and you're glad to pitch in during an emergency, but Imposers make a habit of exploiting you. They are so wound up in whatever they want to do that they are oblivious to anyone else's feelings or needs. They promise to return the favor and never do, but you're not looking for favors. You want them to leave you alone and stop saying that you ought to help them "because that's what friends are for." No friend would be that unfeeling and presumptuous.

Some Imposers put on a helpless act. These poor, dependent souls aren't helpless at all, just crafty in getting you to do their work while they use company time to return a personal phone call or run an "urgent" errand.

You know what they're doing is wrong. You hate being a part of it, but you don't want to hurt their feelings. You have great difficulty saying no to Imposers.

What You're Thinking

I'm so mad at myself for letting Maya put me in this position. I'm getting behind in my own work while I'm answering the requests she's supposed to handle. I thought she just needed an hour or so, but she's been on the phone every day this week with her attorney or witnesses for her trial. I tried to tell her I didn't want to do this anymore. She was so insistent, I couldn't get out of it.

An Imposer's Thoughts

I sure hope the boss doesn't catch me on the phone so much, but I really don't have a choice. I have to take care of personal business, and the only time I can reach these people is during office hours.

STRATEGY

Your goal is to free yourself from doing something you don't want to do. This is especially important if you also believe what you've been asked to do is wrong and you feel torn between helping a colleague and obeying company policy.

1. *Remember that you don't need a reason to refuse a request.* Expressing your regret is sufficient. But if that sticks in your softhearted throat, sandwich your refusal between two compliments or helpful comments.
2. *Practice firm responses at home.* Make a video of yourself and role-play rejections. Critique your performance to ensure that you come across in a calm and polite manner. Just because you think your colleague is being lazy or inconsiderate, that doesn't give you the right to be rude.
3. *Suggest more appropriate ways to deal with the problem.* Consider how else the needs of the Imposer might be met in a more responsible fashion. Place that responsibility back where it belongs—on the Imposer—without showing signs of hostility or sarcasm.

TACTICAL TALK

You: *(Simple refusal, no reason.) I'm sorry, Maya, I can't help you today.*

Or: *(Practiced response.) Gee, Maya, I can see you're really in a bind, but I can't help out because I'm so far behind in my own work. Maybe Sebastian isn't too busy. Why not ask him?*

Or: *Maya, you really do need some help. How are you going to get your project done by the deadline? The only time you can make your personal calls is during office hours, which is strictly forbidden. If you get caught, you're in big trouble. But there is an answer. Discuss the problem with the boss. Arrange for a few hours off to take care of a personal emergency and offer to make up the time later on.*

Tip: Refuse to be used. You're not really helping dependent people by supplying the crutch instead of making them face their responsibilities. And you're not helping yourself by remaining silent when you're being unreasonably imposed upon. If you're meek and don't speak, you won't like yourself. The anger within you builds and sometimes explodes, and then you find yourself apologizing to peers, friends, and family. Speak up!

DUCK AND DIVERS

Duck and Divers plan with you, then leave you holding the bag to face the consequences.

These colleagues are cowards. They support you as long as they think the issue is popular, then they cut and run, leaving you alone to take the responsibility. You thought they were your friends, and their behavior hurts.

While there's no excusing people who encourage you to go out on a limb and then saw it off, you do have to face the fact than an office friend differs from a social friend. Selfish interests may get in the way, for example, when you both go after the same top assignment or promotion. So, as long as it seems safe, the office friends agree with you on what should be done. Then if the boss opposes the idea, or it doesn't meet group approval, your colleagues start ducking and diving before you even know what hit you. You feel pretty foolish being out there by yourself when you claimed to be speaking for "a few of us" who had this brainstorm.

What You're Thinking

I'm going to find a way to get even with Skylar and Glen for setting me up. When we talked about presenting a leadership workshop for our supervisors, they were all for it and promised to back me up if I presented the plan at the management meeting. Then when the boss started frowning and the others started complaining about the costs and time away from work, Skylar and Glen joined the chorus. I felt like an idiot, but I'll get back at them.

A Duck and Diver's Thoughts

Caleb has no antenna working for him. He should have sensed from the boss's expression that this was no time to bring up a proposal that would cost unbudgeted money. He never knows when to back off. The timing was wrong. There was no way I was going to stick my neck out.

STRATEGY

When you put your fingers in a hot oven, you might get burned. But you still have to use it, and so the next time you use an oven mitt. Similarly, you still have to work with the Duck and Divers. Getting even with your colleagues won't help. Your goal is to protect yourself from any such future injuries with better preparation.

1. *Plan to negotiate.* Decide in advance where you perceive the power lies among your peers and how much influence each of you has. What is it that you want, and what are you willing to exchange for something they want?

2. *Stay in control.* When you want your concept to be presented as a joint effort, act rather than react. Send a detailed plan to all involved by email. Receive confirmation by email from each contributor before moving forward. Decide how each of you will participate. If you alone are doing the speaking, introduce your fellow planners before you start your talk. That way, no one can back out of the commitment.

TACTICAL TALK

You: *Skylar and Glen, I'm glad you like this idea because I think your opinions carry weight in influencing the others. You've added some good touches, and I'd like to present this as a joint proposal to recognize the part you've played in making it saleable.*

Or: *I've incorporated your thinking into this outline that we can submit along with the presentation.*

> **Tip:** Don't float a shaky idea until you've organized a raft of support. Before presenting a joint proposal, prepare it in written form and get each participant's approval by email.

OPERATORS

Operators, with their charming gift of gab, convince you to do their bidding.

These colleagues are so smooth, you don't realize you've been duped by a con artist. Operators are glib, slick, and crafty. Their reasons are so compelling, you readily agree to do what they ask.

Sometimes they've violated company policy and want you to send some emails or to intercede with the boss on their behalf. Sometimes they see a potential career advantage and pump you for information that is supposed to be kept confidential. Whatever they're after, you go along because you believe you're serving some good purpose. You tell yourself the end result excuses the questionable method.

After a time, it dawns on you that you feel downright uncomfortable being mixed up in somebody else's wheeling and dealing.

What You're Thinking

Stella is asking me to tell the boss that there were extenuating circumstances that led her to violate the policy. I can see where Stella might have thought she was justified, and I know I need Stella to help me with my projects. I sure hate being in the middle of this, but how can I refuse?

An Operator's Thoughts

When the boss spelled out our company's objectives, he did say that we should stay clear of certain contacts. But I don't think he understood the true picture. If it had worked out, I'd be a hero today. I've got to scrounge up some support from coworkers the boss respects, especially people whose work benefits from my talent.

STRATEGY

Your goal is to avoid being drawn into an Operator's shrewd and perhaps unscrupulous schemes.

1. *Ask a lot of questions.* While Operators are clever and quick-witted, they'd rather deal with colleagues who don't require protracted explanations. If your initial gut feeling is that the request might be improper or unethical, it probably is.

2. *Offer the proper kind of assistance.* Don't take on somebody else's work or problem as your own. Acknowledge areas where they've been successful. Ask more questions to focus the Operator's attention on acceptable alternatives that are available. Then they can work out their own problems.

3. *Refuse future favors from Operators.* The price you pay may be eternal subservience or worse.

TACTICAL TALK

You: *Stella, did the boss specifically tell you not to make these contacts?. . .How many did you make?. . .What exactly were you trying to accomplish?. . .Why did you feel you couldn't go through regular channels?*

Or: *What other options do you think might be open?. . .Have you considered making a formal request?. . .Are there others in the group who feel as you do?. . .Have you tried brainstorming with them?*

Or: *Tony, why do you need this information?. . .How are you going to use it? I think both of us would get into a lot of trouble if I opened the files, and you don't want that to happen, do you?*

> **Tip:** Dispel the spell that Operators cast over you. By asking pointed questions, you'll find the sorcerer's black magic takes on a new and revealing light.

Counteracting shrewd and manipulative colleagues requires honesty and candor. Some people lock themselves into stressful situations by keeping still, believing, as Cervantes wrote, "a closed mouth catches no flies." That may be so, but a closed mouth also offers no relief from people who take advantage of you.

Stop worrying about hurting the feelings of colleagues who exploit you. You won't. You can refuse without being rude. You may be able to show them a better way. If they don't want to listen, they'll just try to trick the next person into doing what they want done.

CHAPTER 12

WHEN YOUR SUBORDINATES ARE EXPLOITIVE

- Bootlickers
- Snitchers
- Rumormongers

Some workers try to manipulate bosses much the way children try to manage their parents. Among the more popular tactics is currying favor by flattery in order to be assigned a certain task or to get out of doing one.

Other subordinates take advantage of your need to know what's going on by telling tales on their coworkers. Some workers will purposely spread rumors to make themselves seem more important. While you oppose snitching and personal gossiping, just by being there you are enmeshed in office politics, whether or not you want to be part of the political process.

You're faced with having to differentiate between views colored by manipulating maneuvers and news that's valid business information you should be tuned in on.

BOOTLICKERS

Bootlickers fawn over you, seek favors, and tell you what you want to hear.

Bootlicker subordinates will say anything to get your attention and win your support. They use insincere compliments to try to get you to like them. They cling like parasites, getting others to do their work. They're not lazy or helpless, but they are manipulative.

They want to get noticed and are using the wrong means to catch your eyes and your ears. If you think these workers have potential worth developing, help them build up their confidence by reducing their dependency.

What You're Thinking

Bobbie keeps saying how happy she is to be working for me, what a wonderful boss I am, how much she's learning from me, how my leadership has put our division far ahead of the others. Okay, I admit that's what I want to believe. Her flattery sure sounds good, and I'm being taken in. She has managed to twist me around her finger, slipping out of tasks I assigned to her. When I asked her to go with Jeff to see the client, she claimed she needed more time to work on the annual report instead. She'd just complain incessantly if I forced her to go, so I conceded. I think she's managing me more than I'm managing her. How can I get her to do what I want without creating animosity?

A Bootlicker's Thoughts

The boss really fell for that line about his leadership style and the way I tied that into our annual report. I had to say something because there's no way I'm going to another meeting with the client. The boss really is good, but he's a softie. I certainly want to remain in his good favor and move up the ladder as he advances with the company.

STRATEGY

Your goal is to regain control of your team.

1. *Ask yourself the right questions—not non-questions.* Stop going around in circles, wondering what to do to avoid resentment. Ask questions for which there are answers, such as, "What soft skills should we be helping our employees develop?" Adaptability and dependability are two of them.

2. *Be firm and resolute when making assignments.* Get to the point, without a preamble. As long as you're polite and reasonable, subordinates understand their survival depends upon doing what the boss asks. If, for instance, you need someone's expertise at a given time, you make the decision based on a broader picture than the worker has. If the subordinate's response is unexpected and you want to modify your request, instead of giving an instant reply, say you'll get back to him or her a little later.

3. *Build the Bootlicker's confidence.* Provide opportunities for them to develop in areas where they experienced success. Encourage discussion. Be there, but empower them to solve their own work problems. Give frequent feedback, sharing your view of how they come across and how they can improve and why they'd want to.

4. *Teach Bootlickers the proper way to praise.* Show by your own example how to compliment someone's work, saying something specific about the performance rather than making a general

comment about the person, and stating why you believe that was important. Develop a system for acknowledging good work both publicly and privately.

5. *Be constructive when criticizing.* Accentuate the positive; avoid threats, bribes, and comparisons with coworkers. Talk about why something angers you rather than accusing them of deliberately jeopardizing your operation.

TACTICAL TALK

You: *Bobbie, I know your time constraints, but it's important for our team that you and your experience be at that meeting. We'll discuss your workload later. It's also important for you. You've had some good results with presenting our case, and I'd like for you to get more exposure.*

Or: *We agree you should have a reasonable workload. Let's examine the alternatives and see what we can do instead.*

Or: *Bobbie, I know you want to move up and I want to help. So I think you should be aware of certain perceptions others have about you. . . . I get upset when I realize we may lose an important contract if we don't have the right presentation.*

> **Tip:** When your subordinates are exploitive, help them build their self-confidence. Also check yourself to make sure they're not reacting to your manipulating them: Do you try to get them to do something by making them feel guilty? Do you expect too much? Are you making deals ("I'll do this for you if you do that for me")?

SNITCHERS

Snitchers are squealers who tattle on their peers and spread malicious stories about them.

Sometimes Snitchers tell tales because they're jealous or vengeful. It's a childish way of trying to make themselves appear better by making a coworker look bad. Subordinates often resort to squealing because they feel frustrated at being unable to advance from their present level.

They take on the role of informant, hoping to gain an advantage when some position does open up. If that's the case, you have to tighten your managerial reins. Look at your existing or nonexisting measurable objectives, how you are rating and rewarding good performance, and the quality of discussions with each of your workers.

When faced with malicious faultfinding, look beyond the gossip to the forces that are producing it. Why are these workers feeding the grapevine or coming to you with their stories? What power struggles are going on? Are the results inconsequential, or are innocent people being harmed?

What You're Thinking

Jackson told me a couple of things about Tim that could possibly be important for me to know. According to the grapevine, Tim and his wife are having some problems. Maybe this wouldn't be a good time for Tim to take on a new and challenging assignment. On the other hand, maybe Jackson told me that so I'd ask him, instead of Tim, to do that highly visible job. Jackson also complained that Tim was late with the monthly figures. Tim is too good a worker to let this go by. I'd better have a talk with him to find out what is really going on here.

A Snitcher's Thoughts

I think I planted that tidbit about Tim pretty well, offering it as a possible explanation for Tim's work not being up to the usual high standard. If the boss goes by the water cooler, she'll hear the same thing. It doesn't take long to get wall-to-wall coverage on fresh gossip.

STRATEGY

Your goal is to sort the information you get from Snitchers. You have to separate harmful, spiteful gossip from useful intelligence data.

1. *Teach tattletales to solve their own problems.* In considering jealous backstabbing, ask yourself why they are trying to use you. Have you become the indirect means for dealing with problems they refuse to face directly? Force subordinates to take responsibility for themselves. Don't get caught in the infighting.

2. *Determine whether you need to change procedures that might be encouraging tattletales.* You don't have to reveal your source when following up on some report that was given to you, such as a worker who's having a problem or a customer who was dissatisfied.

3. *Be alert for clues to potential patterns, problems, and changes.* Go to lunch with your team often. Listen when your subordinates talk to each other. Stay tuned. You'll unearth what's really going on in your organization that you ought to be thinking about or planning for. When you're at a team meeting, keep your ears open and watch to see who is talking to whom. Chat with anyone who's in touch with the many levels of your organization.

You: *Jackson, it seems to me the problem is between you and Tim, and I don't want to get caught in the middle. But it is important that you work something out, because we can't have petty squabbling interfere . . .*

Or: *Tim, are you facing some difficulty? I noticed you were late with the monthly figures. It isn't like you to be late with anything. Is there anything I can do to help?*

> **Tip:** If there's a lot of snitching going on around your office, look at how you're motivating your subordinates. They may feel dead-ended and resort to being informants to carve a place for themselves when a new position does come to pass. Weigh what's being said against what the squealer has to gain by telling this to you. Lead by example by steering clear of gossip and focusing only on relevant business information.

RUMORMONGERS

Rumormongers are gossips who spread unverified facts of questionable origin.

Rumormongers, like Snitchers, also spread stories. However, their focus is broader than personal mudslinging. Their intent is to gain attention for themselves by aggrandizing untrue or partly true messages. They often embroider the story, filling in the blanks to make it appear more important or believable or how they think it "should" be. They may go the other way, forgetting details, remembering only vivid parts, and distorting the facts by omitting vital information.

Rumormongers interpret what happened or is about to happen based on their own interests. Their own experiences, expectations, and views color and limit how they report a situation. The difficulty for you is in deciding which story or how much of a story to believe.

What You're Thinking

Uh-oh, here comes "Loose Lips" Lucy. I wonder what she's going to tell me today. I have to pay attention to what she's saying, even though she gets only part of it right. Things may be happening in the company that might affect my department.

A Rumormonger's Thoughts

That may be an important piece of information I heard from my friend in the manager's office. Why would those bigwigs have had a secret meeting? I'd better tell the boss about it right away. Now, let me try to remember what I heard. . . .

STRATEGY

You never know whether a Rumormonger is telling a story that is true, partly true, or entirely false. You goal is to listen and sift information for parts that can be verified and, if necessary, acted upon.

1. *Keep your door open.* Encourage constant contact with your people to hear what's going on. Let Rumormongers come in and talk to you. You want to know about problems that can affect your operation before everybody else does.
2. *Cut short discussions that are obviously meaningless and spiteful gossip.* Stop meaningless gossip, and definitely do not participate in it. Respond in a disinterested, noncommittal manner.

3. *Ask Rumormongers a lot of questions.* Try to find out where the story originated and how reliable the information is. Determine whether this is a first- or seventh-hand account.

4. *Check the facts.* How much is true and how much has been distorted? What are the dangers of acting—or not acting—on this information immediately?

TACTICAL TALK

You: *That's an interesting story, Lucy. Where did you hear it? Who told you that? Who told that to her? Do we have any evidence that such a meeting took place? Are they preparing any sort of report?*

Or: *Lucy, I'm trying to track down a rumor that could be a bombshell, and you're the one who'd know what is really happening. I was told that. . . . Can you confirm that? Well, I'd like to suggest that the boss issue a statement before this wild rumor goes any further.*

> **Tip:** You can listen to Rumormongers without condoning idle gossip. It's important to keep your ear to the ground and find out what is going on that might influence your part of the world. But as with any rumor, you have to trace it, verify it, and deal with the reality.

Staying on top of the latest information is an important part of your job. Some subordinates try to manipulate you with flattery. Others dangle bits and pieces of news you can use. Don't accept these messages at face value. Question the motivation. Dig for the source. Verify everything. And make sure that you always lead by example—with honesty, candor, and transparency.

PART FIVE

Dealing with Rude or Abrasive People

Ruder and cruder describes a major change in the workplace. Employees who have been interviewed recently say incivility has worsened. They point to more insensitive, inconsiderate, insolent, insulting, and irreverent behavior.

Rudeness is a vicious cycle that starts at the top and eventually permeates every strata of the organization. When management ignores the problem, it faces significant losses in profit, production, and the retention of good workers.

Some point to the newer technologies (email, text messaging, virtual meetings, etc.) as depriving us of face-to-face contact. It's easier to insult people when they're not looking you in the eye. Others say today's quick pace bears some blame. Everyone's in a hurry. Some are so terribly overloaded, they don't even stop to say good morning.

Part of the problem is generational. In some organizations, individuals spanning four separate generations might work on the same team. Differences in speaking patterns, values, and approaches toward work and working affect the success of cross-generational work teams. For instance, a more experienced worker might take offense to the casual attire and attitude of a Millennial. And the Millennial might be offended that the Baby Boomer doesn't want to try out the latest technology.

Your bosses or colleagues or workers probably don't know they rub others the wrong way. It's tricky to remain polite in this more relaxed atmosphere, without having new guidelines as to what is and isn't appropriate language.

CHAPTER 13

WHEN YOUR BOSS IS DISCOURTEOUS

- **Clods**
- **Ridiculers**
- **Condescenders**

Discourteous bosses don't even try to understand anything from your point of view. You and other workers become nonpeople, there solely to produce the company's product or service. They show no respect for your thinking or your feelings.

Of course, we all have bad days. Occasionally, the best bosses snap, scowl, and scream at the innocent. If you can't ride with the tide, if you let your feelings of self-worth go up and down with the boss's good and bad moods, look within yourself for the cause of the problem.

On the other hand, if you have a boss who is habitually abrasive and emotionally abusive, learn to restore some respect for yourself.

CLODS

Clods are insensitive, inconsiderate bosses who ride roughshod over your feelings.

You had set aside certain important items to discuss as you eagerly awaited your private weekly meeting with your boss (a ritual that was the boss's idea). You're trying to get some advice or make a point, and the boss keeps interrupting you to check her email or to answer her phone. The precious scheduled time has just evaporated.

Perhaps the boss has her head down, nodding as you speak, while she's reading an "urgent" email instead of looking at you and giving you her full attention. Are you boring her? Isn't she interested in what you're saying? Of course she is. But by trying to do two things at once, she fails to recognize her rude insensitivity as well as her decreasing effectiveness as a manager.

At other times your boss makes changes that directly affect your work and neglects to tell you about them. You have to hear the news from someone else. It's embarrassing, as well as undercutting, not to know the latest decision made about a team you're supposed to be managing.

What You're Thinking

I might as well be a piece of furniture for all the notice the boss pays to what I'm saying. She certainly is a thoughtless individual. Look at this budget. She reallocated a lot of funds originally intended for my project. Granted, she has every right to do that. But couldn't she have warned me that this was coming? Why do I always have to read these things in an email or hear them through the grapevine?

A Clod's Thoughts

Let's see. This morning I have three separate meetings with staff people, which should be pretty much routine, and a stack of emails to answer. Some important calls should be coming in with information I need on the Clarion decision, and Ron has to drop by to give me the thumbs-up on the new deal.

STRATEGY

Your boss is so product and profit focused, she doesn't see her staff as individuals. Your goal is to get her to show you the respect you deserve. Remain calm and firm, and keep your remarks simple.

1. *Remain polite; don't compete with the rudeness.* When someone is being impolite (talking to someone else during "your" time, texting while you're speaking, and so on), excuse yourself and leave, or at least offer to come back at another time.

2. *Ask questions.* This lets you know if the other person is listening to you and also rekindles her interest by getting her to express herself. To maintain that interest, keep your comments as succinct as possible.

3. *Explain the problem in terms of the trouble it creates for the boss.* You can't come right out and call your boss a coldhearted, mindless idiot, but you can show how it is to her advantage to have better communication with her people.

TACTICAL TALK

You: *Boss, you're obviously too busy for us to continue. Let's reschedule at a time that's more convenient for you.*

Or: *Boss, I smell trouble ahead. I need your undivided attention for just five minutes so that you can avoid a crisis and possible revenue loss.*

Or: *Boss, there seems to be a communication problem in our department. I know you'd want me to bring it to your attention so that we can correct it. . . .*

Tip: You won't get respect until you expect it. When rude bosses bruise your ego, forget your fantasies about how to get even. Concentrate on being treated politely, with attention to your thinking and your feelings. Don't sit still while bosses walk all over you, but don't let them see you cry or you won't get the critical feedback that you need. You can always get up and leave. If you're bypassed on essential information, ask for it. Start by respecting yourself.

RIDICULERS

Ridiculers belittle you with taunting wit that scarcely covers their true intent.

Some rude bosses use sarcasm to thinly veil their criticism. They mistakenly think this brand of humor makes it easier for you to accept a correction. But you don't sense any jokes coming across. You just feel sharp jabs. You try to laugh when you really want to hide and sulk.

Other bosses pretend to be teasing you in order to hide their impatience, saying things like, "Only my ninety-year-old grandfather would take so much time to get me this information. Can't you do a basic Google search?"

Good-natured teasing you can take. Criticism about your work you can handle. But these bosses taunt and humiliate you with personal attacks, especially in front of other people. To you, the implication is clear: They're telling the immediate world that they think you're an imbecile.

What You're Thinking

Why does the boss have to use sarcasm to tell me I'm doing something wrong? Why doesn't she come right out and say that I should be doing something another way? I think she has to keep proving to herself that she's worthy of the job, and that she's better and smarter than the rest of us. There I was, talking to my client, and the boss steps in and takes over, making a joke about how long it takes me to do the paperwork. The infuriating put-down made me appear incompetent to the client.

A Ridiculer's Thoughts

I may be the youngest manager in the company, but I got this job for a reason. I'm the best when it comes to closing a deal. Brenda's good, but she'd be there till next winter if I didn't step in.

STRATEGY

You sense that the boss's sarcasm is sending you a message. Your objective is to get the boss to become more straightforward in telling you what she wants done and how she wants it done.

1. *Schedule a private meeting with the boss.* Be up-front in admitting that you felt a little disturbed and want to clear the air. Do not criticize the boss for ridiculing you. Be professionally matter-of-fact so that you don't sound like a crybaby.

2. *Ask the boss to explain what she meant by the remarks.* Open the door to receive good, constructive comments. Don't be afraid to share why the approach you used worked for you in the past. Still, be

receptive to new suggestions. Listen and demonstrate a drive for continuous improvement.

You: *Boss, I know how important it is to you that we close every sale. I understand your apprehension when someone else is doing a closing that you can do so well yourself. But when you take over in the middle of my closing, the client loses respect for the company, which is embarrassing for both of us.*

Can we discuss the best way to proceed? Would you prefer that I turn over my client to you at the point of closing? Or maybe you could show me a better way to handle it myself?

> **Tip:** Often, bosses who utilize humor to correct or criticize their workers see themselves as stand-up comics. Unless you indicate otherwise, they will keep thinking that their sarcasm is a well-received way to soften an attack.

CONDESCENDERS

Condescenders patronize and talk down to you, doing you a favor to be with them.

These bosses have an exaggerated opinion of themselves and a devaluated opinion of others. Haughty and snooty, they are intellectual snobs who tacitly permit you to join the discussion. Then the Condescenders ignore your ideas, zapping you with put-downs as they downplay your suggestions.

They are quick to grasp the full implications of a problem and faster than you are at seeing solutions. They are also insulting when they allow you to do something on your own: "This is an easy job. Jose can handle it."

What You're Thinking

My boss is really very smart about the business, but he never learned to act with tact. Everybody puts up with his abrasive manner because he gets results. I guess I'm fortunate that his rude comments aren't directed solely at me. He shares his arrogance among all of us. I make a point and he adds another aspect to it.

Fine, but why does he have to preface it with, "What Jose was trying to say is . . ."? I am perfectly capable of expressing myself, so why do I let him make me feel like an idiot?

A Condescender's Thoughts

That was sheer genius, the way I got the board to go along with the proposal. Anticipating every reaction, I had all the facts and figures to allay their concerns. My staff is still panting, trying to keep up with me. I wish my staff would stop offering me their ideas after they get themselves into a mess. It's their distorted thinking that brings on the problems in the first place, and they need my clear analysis to bail them out. I must remind them before the next crisis to bring me only the problem, not their misguided solutions.

STRATEGY

It's safe to assume that these bosses were applauded for accomplishments all their lives, and no one ever bothered to teach them humility. They believe they are excellent administrators. It's unlikely that anything you say will change them or soften and mellow their overbearing rudeness. What you can change is your reaction to their lack of tact. Also, you can guard against a possible unwarranted attack.

1. *Choose to dwell on how good and talented you are.* Bosses can't make you feel bad about your self-worth unless you let them. In time, you won't even hear the tactless comments. You'll be too busy thinking and planning along with the boss for your next success.

2. *Gently remind the boss you play a part in what he's accomplishing.* You want him to appreciate your trying, even if you don't quite measure up to his excessive standards. Prepare your remarks in advance of your staff meetings. Use progress reports to deftly and delicately tell the boss how capable you are, *quantifying* the efforts you expended. Numbers make a greater impression than adjectives. Let everyone bask in the glory of the finished product or service.

3. *Pay close attention to the office grapevine.* An arrogant boss is an unlikely candidate for sharing the blame with you when things go wrong. Keep on top of developments to avoid becoming the fall guy. Don't wait for your problem to mushroom into a crisis. Ask early for the boss's help, but wait until he asks before you suggest solutions.

TACTICAL TALK

Boss: *The next agenda item is the satisfaction survey. Jose, I don't suppose you were able to—*

Jose: *Boss, as you know, this is a huge undertaking. We must move quickly and with quality to. . . . According to our survey, 64 percent said that. . . . And 87 percent expressed a willingness to. . . .*

Boss: *Jose was surprisingly close to what we need, but he needs to face the reality of—*

Jose: *It's your call, boss. Consider, however, that the costs will increase by roughly 22 percent if we wait until. . . .*

Tip: The bosses' condescending remarks will diminish in proportion to the amount of increased respect you are able to earn. They're clever and conceited; you can be clever and considerate. Be ready with facts that you've double- and triple-checked for accuracy. Acknowledge that they're the bosses, but when you do get the go-ahead, move quickly and confidently—and keep them informed.

The most important point about dealing with rudeness is that you don't have to take it, even from your boss, even when you fear your job is on the line. No matter the gender or age of the offender, the first step is believing that you deserve respect, because you won't get it until you expect it.

Then you can respectfully show a boss how he or she benefits by being polite. If you think bosses are using rude remarks to mask complaints, they probably are. Find the trouble and correct it. You can dispel rudeness by being up-front and minding your own manners. Treat others the way you want to be treated.

CHAPTER 14

WHEN YOUR COLLEAGUES ARE DISCOURTEOUS

- **Interrupters**
- **Left-Handed Complimenters**
- **Insulters**

With peers, as with bosses, you can't afford to feud with the rude. That approach only drains your time and energy, escalates the problem, and doesn't help you get what you want. Nor can you accept the rudeness, or you'll feel yourself getting increasingly agitated. You want to stop the discourtesies, but the thought of telling the people you work with every day that they are being rude embarrasses you. So you sit there wondering why they act like juvenile brats.

Some immature coworkers think that it's cool to be "in your face" and that manners were something their parents practiced. Some are brash because they feel insecure. Whether they interrupt your work, make snide remarks, or mind your business for you, recognize the common thread. These egocentric offenders are all so interested in themselves, they are not giving you or your feelings a second thought.

Follow two guidelines to point them in the right direction—honesty and courtesy.

INTERRUPTERS

Interrupters rudely break into your discussion, burst into your office un-invited, or pester you with emails, texts, and phone calls.

What irritates you most about Interrupters is that they nibble away at your peak productive hours. They plop down at your desk during the time you had set aside to work on a potentially big project, or they continuously FaceTime you when you are working from home. After you finish their chats, you can't recapture the thoughts that were inter-rupted.

Almost as annoying is when they waste your time at meetings by getting the discussion off track. They speak in stage whispers to fellow workers when you're trying to hear the boss's comments on the latest marketing report. They never let you finish the point you're making.

Usually, Interrupters don't know they are regarded as pests or an-noyances. Their crime is being self-centered and inconsiderate. Their punishment, eventually, is being ignored. In the meantime, your stress level is climbing to the breaking point.

What You're Thinking

Dominic seems to have made me his new best friend. I'm glad to talk to him when I have the time, but he keeps interrupting my work by popping in and out of my office and by texting me when he can't find me in person. I've got to find a way to put a stop to this without hurting his feelings.

An Interrupter's Thoughts

Matt is a great guy with so much experience. He's been a real help talking to me the past few months on this new job. Today the boss sent me a new production figure that somehow doesn't seem right. I'll call Matt and ask him what he thinks about it and how I should handle it. Better yet, I'll stop by his office right now.

STRATEGY

Your aim is to break your colleague's thoughtless behavior pattern. To do so, you have to interrupt the Interrupter. But handle with care or your Interrupter will become antagonistic, and this could lead to other problems.

1. *Be polite when you do the interrupting.* Smile, start with the person's name, and couple your friendly tone with sensitive phrases. Be considerate even though your Interrupter is not.
2. *Be straightforward in explaining why you can't be interrupted now.* People understand when you're under pressure. Simply explain that you have a deadline, a report to prepare, or pre-conference materials to gather. If you don't have time to talk right then but want to continue, suggest a time that's mutually convenient.
3. *Snatch back control when your conversation is intercepted.* Interrupt your Interrupter for a minute or two to finish making your point.
4. *Stop the rambler with sharply focused comments and questions.* Bring the discussion back to the stated purpose. Politely break in to summarize an Interrupter's unending monologue.
5. *Discourage Interrupters from coming in and staying in your office.* Reposition your desk so that a passerby can't catch your eye. Limit the number of chairs and stack them with reports or books. Stand up when an Interrupter comes in, and remain standing.

6.   *Don't jump to respond to every text or to answer every FaceTime call.* Only treat as urgent those calls and texts that truly need your immediate attention. Respond to nonurgent messages when you have a break in your day.

TACTICAL TALK

You: *Dominic, hold on a minute. From what you're saying, I think you need to be talking to the boss about this, not me.*

Or: *Dominic, is this really important? I'm trying to get ready for a meeting. If you need more than a minute, we'll have to talk later.*

Or: *I'd like to talk, but I can't now. How about lunch?*

Or: *I'm so glad to hear from you, but I'm on my way out. I'll call back as soon as I can.*

Or: *Yes, that may be so, but please let me finish. We have to follow this route because. . . .*

Or: *We seem to have shifted the topic from the purpose of the meeting. As I understand it, you're saying that. . . . Have I stated your view correctly?*

Or: *I think that about covers it, don't you?*

Or: *Just one more point before you go.*

Or: *I've taken up too much of your time.*

> **Tip:** Interrupters either are not aware or do not care that they are selfishly imposing their needs on others. You can refuse to accept this form of rudeness and yet be gracious yourself. If you're being interrupted and can't think of what to say, remember George Bernard Shaw's observation: "Silence is the most perfect expression of scorn."

LEFT-HANDED COMPLIMENTERS

Left-Handed Complimenters start by praising you and end with a qualifying put-down.

The first time this happens, you're caught off guard. You felt so good about the praises that you didn't realize there might be a negative implication tied to it. A little later, you wonder if you just imagined the slap or if it was an intended sideswipe.

The next time the Left-Handed Complimenter strikes, you know your imagination was not working overtime. The two-sided remark was meant as a jab. Trying not to show signs of being stung, you feel yourself smile and you hear yourself sputter "thanks" while knowing that's not the way you ought to respond. Then you kick yourself for having thanked somebody who just got away with putting you down.

What You're Thinking

I find myself trying to avoid Taylor. I don't know why she's being rude to me, but she seems to delight in building me up and knocking me down at the same time. Maybe I'm getting paranoid. Was there a hidden meaning when she said I'm looking so much better these days? Is that just what young kids say to one another? What's wrong with the way I looked before? And that crack about my report being great—*this* time. I've got enough problems without worrying about her.

A Left-Handed Complimenter's Thoughts

Violet is acting so high-and-mighty these days. I've asked her to go to lunch with me a couple of times, but she's always too busy. She's determined to get ahead of the rest of us. I think she feels entitled to the promotion because she's been here for fifteen years. I resent the way she's causing everybody else to work up to her pace.

STRATEGY

Your goal is to maintain your composure as you seize control of the conversation. In some cases, you may need feedback from your alleged offender before you're sure you are really dealing with a culprit.

1. *Keep your cool and question the intent of the remark.* When called to account for their inappropriate comments, Left-Handed Complimenters duck for cover. They try to blame you for misinterpreting. But they are also less likely to pick on you now that they see you're not so vulnerable as they had believed.

2. *Dig a little deeper for an underlying cause.* What you interpreted as a left-handed compliment may actually be covering hidden resentment or anger toward you. A pleasant confrontation may clear the air.

3. *Divide the remark into two parts: praise and put-down.* Accept with sincerity the compliment that pleased you. Correct or ignore the implied insult.

TACTICAL TALK

Taylor: *That was a great report, Violet. Why can't you do that kind of work all the time?*

Violet: *I'm glad you liked my report. I worked hard on it, as I do on all my projects. The boss tells me he's very pleased with my performance. (Dividing the remark and accepting only the praise.)*

Or:

Taylor: *You're looking so much better these days, Violet.*

Violet: *Thank you, Taylor. But I'm a little confused. In what way do I appear to look better to you?*

Taylor: *Why are you acting so touchy?*

Violet: *What makes you say I'm acting touchy? Taylor, I sense that you may be upset with me. If I've done something to offend you, please tell me so that we can straighten things out.*

> **Tip:** When you sense that colleagues are using disguised jabs to inflame your feelings, stop to verify your assumption. Once convinced, you free yourself to respond pleasantly to the complimentary part while ignoring or tossing back the negative aspect.

INSULTERS

Insulters sling intentionally defiant remarks that feel like a slap in the face.

While you may wonder if you've been put down by Left-Handed Complimenters, there's no doubt about it with Insulters. These affronts are issued on purpose, and you don't know why.

Sometimes Insulters are reacting to your lack of appreciation, like the time your colleague did so much to help you on your presentation and felt she deserved more than your curt, unfeeling, one-line "thank you" text. You may be feeling rushed and self-absorbed, unaware that coworkers regard your snubbing them in the hallway as deliberately unfriendly.

Or perhaps it's the liberties you take when speaking. Feeling uninhibited, you may not stop to think how your remarks and jokes can be perceived as demeaning and hurtful.

What You're Thinking

Why is Tyrone bent out of shape? He's hitting me with one insult after another. He snaps at everything I say to him. He seems to be overly sensitive. I think he's got a chip on his shoulder. I would like to get along better, since we have to work together. How can I nip this in the bud?

An Insulter's Thoughts

I'm mad about Cary's ongoing commentary. I pretend not to be angry, but I'm really furious. It's obvious she hasn't learned how to listen when I speak to her. I realize that we come from different backgrounds. That shouldn't be a problem, but she's never tried to understand the differences in our cultures. All I want from her is a little respect.

STRATEGY

Your aim is to stop the open warfare. First find the cause, then you can correct it. Usually there's at least a grain of truth in the insult.

1. *Ask, then pay close attention to the answer.* Conflict is positive and necessary when you're getting an issue out in the open; it's destructive when accompanied by inappropriate behavior.
2. *Convince Insulters that they'll benefit if they're polite.* Conversely, point out that they could damage their careers if they're not.
3. *Agree on boundaries you can both accept.* Adopt a do-and-don't policy. Talk it out. What actions and words are offensive to Insulters that you will now avoid? What method will Insulters substitute to react to your perceived offense?

TACTICAL TALK

Cary: *Tyrone, what's going on here? Why do you keep insulting me?*

Tyrone: *You don't know? That's because you're so self-centered. You don't even want to find out how offensive your ethnic comments can be.*

Cary: *I didn't realize—*

Tyrone: *(Interrupting.) Well, it's time you did.*

Cary: *Then let's talk about this. You may not be aware how ongoing quarreling can put both our careers in jeopardy. If I admit I've been careless and insensitive, will you admit that insulting each other is no way to resolve our differences?*

Tyrone: *Okay, what do you suggest?*

Cary: *Well, we could work out a system. You tell me why some expressions anger you. Make a list for me of words to avoid. And when you feel offended, call me on it instead of tossing darts in my face.*

> **Tip:** Don't just brood when you think someone's rude. Stop accepting behavior you don't want to tolerate. Calmly confront. Otherwise, if you try to swallow real or imagined insults, you'll choke on them.

Rude colleagues wear many faces. The abrasiveness of their inconsiderate behavior becomes increasingly irritating. It's like wearing a tight shoe until the day a blister sidelines you. Don't wait to erupt before you take action. You don't have to continue taking it, and you don't have to lose your cool. If you respond with rudeness, you're letting their bad behavior rub off on you. Be straightforward and polite while standing your ground.

CHAPTER 15

WHEN YOUR SUBORDINATES ARE DISCOURTEOUS

- **Free Spirits**
- **Snippy Talkers**
- **Defiers**
- **Needlers**

When bosses are disrespectful and deflating, workers say they're arrogant. When subordinates behave like that, supervisors call them impudent and presumptuous.

Surprisingly enough, this discourteous attitude is sometimes triggered by bosses who are too good to be true: bosses who go out of their way to be nice and considerate; bosses who are careful to let their subordinates solve their own problems.

Workers who are looking for direction from above and not getting it may constantly feel they're in a state of crisis. They may, for example, need a clear division of who's doing what steps in the operation, by what dates. When their bosses are "so nice" that subordinates can't complain to them, their frustration may manifest itself by workers being snippy or defiant.

If being too nice isn't your problem, your rude workers may be feeling pressure from some other source and simply not know how to cope. They take out their anxiety or anger on you or their fellow workers. Whatever the cause, you want to reduce the tension in the office.

FREE SPIRITS

Free Spirits—irreverent, animated, impulsive, and outspoken—are so candid that they seem tactless, disrespectful, and offensive.

Primarily, we're looking at a generation gap separating boss and worker. What you see as impudent, Free Spirits see as enthusiastic. You think they're blunt, brazenly impertinent, and sometimes gross; they think you're dull, uptight, and what their folks used to call old-fashioned fuddy-duddies.

While you wonder if Free Spirits are the product of doting parents or a lack of parental guidance, you're really concerned about what you should do when customers are offended by their responses and reactions.

What You're Thinking

The greeting "What's up?" is so common today that it's no longer objectionable. But young adults like Aiden and some of the others ought to be more professional and less presumptuous, especially when they're not talking to one of their peers. While I appreciate his talent, he's going to need more than tech savvy. His stream of lively, coarse, bold expressions is crossing the line of acceptable speech into unintentional rudeness. He shows a lack of judgment that I'm afraid will have consequences for this office as well as for his future.

A Free Spirit's Thoughts

The boss is so tense and uncool. She winces at my forward approach. Sure, it's an unrestrained and frank style, but it's friendly and animated.

It shows my honesty and openness. I believe that's what customers are really looking for. This is quality work. It rocks. I'm so good at what I do. There's a demand for my type of skills. If she doesn't like it, tough! Other companies will want me.

STRATEGY

Your goal is to find a way to make two obviously divergent views more compatible.

1. *Latch onto every opportunity.* Listen carefully to what the Free Spirits say and you will find an opening to start a discussion. If you switch and rephrase your thoughts as a question, you're not jamming your feelings down their throats.

2. *Call a meeting of your group to present your concern.* Report comments you've heard from offended parties. Talk about your wish to help them advance by learning to speak less aggressively and with more dignity. Being courteous doesn't rule out being friendly.

3. *Together, decide on a goal.* Make it one that best helps the company and its people. Draw out their thinking, letting each one have a chance to speak. Get their suggestions on how to implement changes that would accomplish the objectives.

TACTICAL TALK

Aiden: *Boss, you know this promotional flyer really sucks. It is so boring, ugh! I mean, nobody will read it.*

You: *(Sensing an opportunity.) Aiden, I need to talk to you now. You've added so much to the office, an infusion of life. People like to be around you.*

Aiden: *You really think so?*

You: *Yes. However, I'm sure you're not aware that when you speak to those who are not of your generation, your usual manner of talking doesn't always appear respectful. I personally find that it is more effective to provide constructive suggestions on how to fix something as opposed to just criticizing it.*

Or: *(To the group.) I've asked you here to report a problem and discuss ways to resolve it. I have two motives—to help the company and to help your individual careers. Some of our long-standing customers have complained that the staff is so aggressively friendly that you're brash. This in-your-face, blunt talk, which is natural when you talk to each other, may be costing us some business. I want to start by hearing your thinking. First, do you also see this as a problem?*

Or: *(After group suggestions.) Thanks, you've given me a lot of good ideas I can look into. I particularly like the idea of sensitivity training. I think you'd be surprised at how much you'd enjoy it.*

> **Tip:** Show the Free Spirits what they'll gain from your game plan. Then try a collaborative approach, letting your workers come up with the solutions.

SNIPPY TALKERS

Snippy Talkers make cutting, impertinent remarks.

These subordinates are miserable and unpleasant to be around. They seem to be aching for an argument. Almost every day, something sets them off soon after they get to work. A late delivery, for instance, might trigger their spending the rest of the day snapping at anyone who walks by.

Since snippy people are concentrating so intently on themselves, they are devoid of common respect and courtesy toward others. They'll toss their sharp verbal darts at a boss as well as a coworker. Because people want to avoid their line of fire, they've been allowed to get away with their taunting remarks.

What You're Thinking

Gabriel's work is very good, and he's certainly demonstrated time and again that he's loyal to me. But I think he's mainly responsible for much of the petty bickering that goes on in this office. He appears to be overprotective of his turf. He can be impatient and insulting and quick to answer me or anyone else with a snippy response, no matter who else happens to be standing there.

A Snippy Talker's Thoughts

I thought I could count on the boss for support. You just can't trust anyone but yourself. How can I do my job if the boss goes over my head and instructs my team? He knows the importance of respecting the chain of command. I feel hurt and angry to be treated in this way. After all I've done for him, the least he could do is back me up.

STRATEGY

When people act snippy, they are probably reacting to something or somebody that made them feel hurt or interfered with their plans. Your goal is to get them to express their anger so you can dig out the real problem and get it resolved.

1. *Reexamine your management style.* Why doesn't your subordinate feel free to talk to you about whatever is bugging him? Have you done something to discourage open communication? What's he afraid of? What does he think is at risk if he is honest with you?

2. *Put the subordinate at ease.* Enable him to talk to you. Make direct eye contact. When he starts talking, just nod or say "I see" to show you comprehend, but don't interrupt him.

3. *Ask questions.* Together, as a team, probe deeper to get at the root of the problem or misunderstanding. If the focus shifts to something your subordinate hadn't considered, and he needs a little more time, suggest meeting soon again.

TACTICAL TALK

You: *Gabriel, you appear to be edgy lately. Let's talk about this. What seems to be the trouble?*

Or: *Well, Gabriel, I'm glad we could clear up the misunderstanding about the chain of command. But what do you think you can do to deal with your anger instead of resorting to snippy remarks? You want to move up, but that kind of behavior will hold you back.*

Tip: Start by assuming that snippy subordinates snap and yap because they're frustrated. They don't know how, or are afraid, to express their feelings. Once you can get them to talk, you're on your way to reducing their anxiety, curtailing their rude behavior, and lowering the level of office tension.

DEFIERS

Defiers are insubordinate and disrespectfully oppose established policy.

You give an order to some subordinates, but they won't do it, don't do it, or delay doing it. They meet each and every assignment by confronting, resisting, challenging, and daring you to do something about their defiance. Eventually the work gets done, but you're worn out from the battle.

What You're Thinking

Tracy deliberately defied my directives. I guess, technically, she's guilty of insubordination, but I couldn't prove it even if I wanted to. Tracy is bound and determined to handle the job her way, even though she creates other problems for us. She keeps arguing with me that her method is better. I've got to put a stop to her undermining my decisions.

A Defier's Thoughts

The boss made me responsible for the project, and I can't do my job if she's going to micromanage me. All those stupid regulations! She's got to set me free to develop this my way.

STRATEGY

Your objective is to get peak performance from all your workers. You want to be reasonable with each one while you keep your eye on the big picture. Your vantage point is not available to your subordinates unless you explain to them how it looks from where you sit.

1. *Check your own attitude.* When workers are defiant, ask yourself if you're being open and playing fair. Do you request or command adherence? Are you explaining the importance of doing something

a certain way? Do you turn mistakes into learning experiences for both of you? Do you resist dangling promises unless you're sure you can keep them?

2. *Get right to the point of your meeting.* Don't beat around the bush or make small talk. Immediately put your subordinate at ease by expressing your desire to continue your working relationship.

3. *Let defiant workers get the gripes off their chests.* Listen carefully. Then bend where you can, but explain why certain procedures must be followed. In a calm, professional manner, ask them to explain why they deliberately disobeyed a directive. Get them to tell you the probable consequences of such actions. Ask them how they plan to deal with the situation.

TACTICAL TALK

You: (*Demanding.*) *I need you to complete the email blast by 10 AM.*

Or: (*Requesting.*) *When will you complete the email blast?*

Or: (*Putting the subordinate at ease.*) *I appreciate the many contributions you have made to the company, and I hope you'll continue making them. But first we have to settle this matter of following orders. . . .*

Tip: A subordinate working on one segment of the operation can't have the same global picture as the boss who's supervising the whole show. While workers' views are invaluable and need to be heard, and while workers have to be free to voice complaints and suggestions, it's still up to you to enforce company policy and important procedures. If you are tactful, both you and your defiant subordinate will feel something's been won in the discussion.

NEEDLERS

Needlers use sharp-pointed humor to provoke and goad you and your team.

It's a delicate matter to criticize the boss, even when you're on the friendliest of terms. Needler subordinates have discovered that masquerading smart, sharp, stinging remarks as humor is one way to complain without being labeled an attacker. They attempt to control a situation without being held accountable for the new direction.

Needlers need an audience such as the rest of the staff or a client. If you protest their antics, Needlers claim it was supposed to be funny. Why aren't you laughing while your ego is being deflated?

What You're Thinking

Xavier knows I really need him, because he's one of our best workers. I tried to show him I was on his side by offering to talk over any problem he was having. When I told him that some people found his needling remarks to be offensive, he just got huffy and defensive. He claims no one in this group has a sense of humor. What am I going to do about this Needler, and how can I get him to stop needling me?

A Needler's Thoughts

Can't they see what's wrong with this picture? You work for years, giving it all you've got, and what do they do? Bring in some young kid from outside instead of promoting from within. I should have that job my new boss has. If I criticize her, I'll get into trouble. But if I disguise my jabs in some needling, I can't be blamed, and I'll be able to let everyone see how inexperienced the new boss really is.

Your objective is to force the Needler to come out of hiding and be open with the criticism. Get right to the point and needle the Needler. To accomplish this, it's essential that you come across as pleasant, friendly, and nonthreatening.

1. *Ask repeatedly for clarification.* Using a variety of phrases, request that the Needler make his criticism clear by being more specific.

2. *Shift the direction.* Get Needlers to move away from jabbing at you and other people and start jabbing at issues. They may be onto something important. Maybe some changes are needed and the procedures have to be reexamined.

3. *Talk privately.* With a smile on your face, let Needlers know their "jokes" didn't accomplish their purpose. Then reassure them that their thinking is invaluable and that you and the rest of the team will be considering their suggestions in depth. Toss them a challenge—some additional problem they might start thinking about how to resolve.

4. *Consider joking back.* Maybe you should lighten up. Consider joking back or smiling silently to take away the Needler's fun.

TACTICAL TALK

You: *(In front of the group.) Xavier, please explain that to us again. What specifically is bothering you about this?. . . What exactly are you objecting to?. . . Some of us don't quite understand the point you are making. . . .*

Or: *(Shrugging off the attack.) Xavier, you may be right.*

Or: *(Laughing.) You've got to be joking!*

Or: *(In private.) Xavier, as you probably guessed, I didn't think your little jokes at the meeting were very funny. But I want you to know that I* *appreciate the fine work you've been doing.* . . . *The trend seems to indicate some expansion in your area. There are at least two problems this could create for us that I'd like you to be thinking about, along with how we might streamline.* . . .

Tip: In trying to disguise criticism with humor, Needlers often miss the point. To win people over, critics should include themselves in the joke. Otherwise, they appear to be sneering or scolding, and that's offensive. With that in mind, you can beat Needlers at their own game. Include yourself in discussing the problem. Also, don't let Needlers see that they get under your skin. Once you start, in a playful, pleasant, and professional manner, the others will join you in needling the Needler.

It takes only a few rude and abrasive workers to make an entire staff feel tense. Sometimes the rude ones openly attack with snide or rebellious remarks. At other times, they try to disguise their criticism through joking, but malicious, insinuations. Since these troublesome subordinates are often good workers, simply subduing them can destroy office morale. To come out with boss and worker both winning, deal with discourtesy right away, without threats. In a professional and friendly manner, ask questions that get to the cause. Let them talk. Once you're paying attention to each other's needs, the tension dissolves and you can start influencing your workers to become more productive.

PART SIX

Dealing with Egotistical or Self-Centered People

According to Benjamin Disraeli, the nineteenth-century British prime minister, "If you talk to people about themselves, they'll listen for hours." Many of us are flattered by attention, and all of us need to be noticed. But egotists go to extremes. A thing has value only according to how it relates to their interests. They think you should be as interested in them as they are in themselves.

Some even want you to keep reliving their past glories. These boring braggarts forget that to maintain acclaim, in the conference room as on the stage or on the football field, you're only as good as your last effort. Their grossly overdeveloped yearning to be admired often turns them into grandstanders. They butt in; they take over. Selfish people are doubly difficult because they can't be team players. They believe that if they help you, you score and they are denied the limelight they desperately seek.

In dealing with egotists, it's natural to want to expose their conceit and self-centeredness. Don't be diverted. Although these bosses, colleagues, and subordinates are troublesome, you can deal with them and still concentrate your energy on your own legitimate goals.

CHAPTER 16

WHEN YOUR BOSS IS SELF-SEEKING

- **Talent Wasters**
- **Brush-Offs**
- **Neglecters**
- **Show-Offs**

Egotistical bosses are centered on themselves. They promote their own interests without concern about how their actions might affect their subordinates. They usurp decisions that should be yours to make. They won't let their managers manage, because they believe they have more expertise.

When bosses won't leave you alone to work, or snip the chain of command by going over your head and directly ordering your subordinates, the help isn't helpful. Egotistical bosses also can be irritating constant checkers, who set no deadlines but email and text you constantly. Some go to the other extreme: They can appear too engrossed in their own quests to bother with you or even be interested in what you're doing.

TALENT WASTERS

Talent Wasters are foolish bosses who won't use, or even consider using, the ideas of those they supervise.

They are cocky, believing they already have all the answers. Not only do they lack desire to listen to those who do the work, they also avoid using such motivators as frequent feedback and delegation of responsibility.

This absence of attention to individual needs and talent—particularly the chance to grow on the job—is a prime reason why Talent Wasters lose good workers.

What You're Thinking

I have some terrific graphic design ideas that all of us could really get excited about. No use. The boss won't hear of any change in the status quo. From him, there's no reaching out, no listening, no way to develop my potential. In this stifling atmosphere, I feel bored and drained when I should be exhilarated. There's more to job satisfaction than a good paycheck. I could be developing rewarding new designs. I don't want to quit, but I will unless I can make things change soon.

A Talent Waster's Thoughts

I've set good goals for the company and I know how we can meet them. I don't need these newbies to tell me their cockeyed ideas. With the salary they get, they should be happy to do things my way. I have to keep close tabs on Jenna. She's itching for more responsibility. But if I turn over some of my tasks to her, there's no telling what wild methods she'd use. Like the old saying goes, if you want something done right, do it yourself.

STRATEGY

Your goal is to persuade your boss to utilize your special skills and appreciate thinking that differs from his own.

1. *Do your homework.* From old-timers, find out why the boss takes certain positions. Search for areas where, in the past, he's been known to bend a little. Take the attitude that you're doing your boss a favor by solving *his* problem.

2. *Put yourself in the boss's shoes.* Figure out what he wants, what's important to him. How could he benefit by availing himself of your strengths and releasing your energy?

3. *Make an appointment with your boss.* Say that you want to discuss an important issue. Stop bombarding him with ideas and telling him what you want. Instead, talk about how you can help him get what he needs. Seek common ground in a calm, low-key, professional manner. Know the financial and nonfinancial costs involved and how, specifically, your idea helps the company.

4. *Consider a short-term, incremental plan.* Instead of asking the boss to risk total commitment or accept a radical change, aim for a plan that would cause him the least amount of embarrassment or loss of esteem. Mention potential unwanted results if your plan isn't adopted. Be specific.

TACTICAL TALK

Boss: *Jenna, if you've come to me with another one of your proposals, I just don't have time to deal with it.*

You: *I understand that, Boss. I wanted to call your attention to a little problem we're having and suggest that you could take a few minutes each week at the end of the meeting to let us fill you in on what we perceive to be happening.*

Boss: *What problem are you talking about?*

You: *Sticking to our schedule when it's taking so long to get client approval of the new designs.*

Boss: *Yes, I'm working on it.*

You: *In my last job, I was utilized quite successfully as a contact person. Perhaps I could become more skilled and valuable to you if you don't have to waste your time on work others can do for you. To get the best out of us, why not take advantage of our individual strengths?*

Boss: *Frankly, I don't know if I can take the chance.*

You: *Well, how about trying this idea for one project—say the Brookfield? Maybe you don't realize this, Boss, but when you let us give something of ourselves to the company, we feel responsible. We then have a vested interest in seeing the company succeed. And you build a loyal, stronger team.*

> **Tip:** When you feel the boss doesn't use your skills and talent, either you didn't speak up or you didn't demonstrate the potential benefits.

BRUSH-OFFS

Brush-Off bosses curtly dismiss you. They are too busy with texts, emails, and phone calls to answer your questions or supply what you need.

Why are these bosses too busy for you? They may not admit it even to themselves, but that's the way they want it. They get bogged down in tasks that others should be doing. Not only aren't you getting the help you need, they also keep others from assisting you. Brush-Off bosses have trouble delegating. For one thing, they believe they can do everything better than everybody else.

Another reason is the fear that if they build up their team and let go of some of the tasks, others will no longer regard them as vital to the operation. As a result, they stifle their own growth. They leave themselves no time to plan important future moves, and they leave you feeling frustrated.

What You're Thinking

I could see the boss resented my asking Sheila for some advice while he was away on Thursday. He's given me responsibility with authority to act. It's always my fault if something goes wrong. I sure needed help. Now I really need those papers before I can proceed, and he keeps dismissing me with "I'll handle it." I understand he's busy, but he doesn't have to be so abrupt and brusque. He shows more respect for the office equipment than he does for me.

A Brush-Off's Thoughts

These people can't conceive the enormous responsibility I have running a large department. You'd think they would show me some consideration and realize that I'm under great pressure. Paul, for example, keeps pestering me for those papers. Why can't he just go away and wait until I'm ready for him?

STRATEGY

Your objective is to complete the jobs you've been assigned. That includes extracting necessary data from a busy boss.

1. *Punt—don't confront.* If you tell the boss he's wrong, he has to defend his ego with a counterattack. So don't even give the

appearance of arguing with him. Often you can turn the ball over to the boss just by asking him his opinion or to make a choice.

2. *Focus on the boss's needs, not yours.* You lose ground if you complain. Force yourself to totally ignore his curt manner, and talk instead about the options he has for enhancing his reputation or achieving his objectives. He's more apt to help you if he views the action as helping himself. Your positive suggestions can light the way.

TACTICAL TALK

You: *Boss, with the Pinocchio Project behind schedule, do you think it would be better to call Mark or email him first, enclosing a list of points we need to know to complete the forms?*

Or: *Boss, I have an idea that can help you free up some time. What if you used the software that gives you a graph like this to indicate the stages of accomplishment?*

> **Tip:** You look better when you help your boss look good. Egotistical bosses worry about the perception their supervisors and colleagues have about their professionalism. Give them ideas that they can claim as their own: "I thought about this yesterday when you were discussing cost-saving procedures. . . ."

NEGLECTERS

Neglecters are indifferent to what is needed and uncaring about inconveniencing you.

Unlike Brush-Off bosses who are too busy to help you, Neglecters are laissez-faire leaders, too disinterested to do anything. They're happy to let you decide the way to go and glad to let you take the blame if you fail. Some won't give you advice or opinions because they refuse to take risks.

Generally, Neglecters are so involved with their own personal pursuits, they don't care enough to see that their subordinates have what's needed to perform well.

What You're Thinking

I can't decide whether the boss won't give me any suggestions because she wants to play it safe or if she just doesn't care enough to make the effort. In the meantime, she's letting me drift, and I feel like I'm going in circles. Should I go ahead and make the decisions myself? How far should I stick my neck out in calling the shots that my boss ought to be calling?

A Neglecter's Thoughts

My workers are capable people. They really don't need me. Besides, they'll learn if they make mistakes. I've got a lot of other things to attend to.

STRATEGY

Your objective is to maneuver around your boss's apparent disinterest and, if possible, turn this situation to your advantage.

1. *First, determine whether the boss is simply forgetful.* She may mean well but can't seem to remember to do what she promised. If so, the boss will regard your asking her about whatever she was supposed to do as your way of expressing interest.

2. *Try to extract a little direction.* Even if it's like pulling teeth, at least make the attempt.

3. *Fill the leadership vacuum.* If your boss neglects to point you in the right direction, move slowly on your own. Decide on a few measurable objectives. Achieve these and set a few more. But

always *keep your boss informed* about what you're doing. Show her your plan before you set your design in motion. Create a paper trail by sending your updates and reports by email.

4. *Enjoy the freedom.* Many would give anything to be in your shoes. Act responsibly and conscientiously.

TACTICAL TALK

You: *Boss, whatever happened when you spoke to Manny about appointing me to serve on the Operations Committee?*

Or: *I sense that you feel I'm veering off course, Boss. What specifically should I adjust? Am I putting emphasis in the wrong place?*

Or: *Here, I've sketched out the stages for achieving my main objectives over the next six months. If you have no objection, I plan to proceed in this way.*

> **Tip:** Establish your own self-protection practices. While Neglecters seem to ignore you, they can resent your doing well by ignoring them. Reduce to writing conversations in which bosses themselves either refuse to commit or tell you to do deeds they should be doing. ("Attached is a synopsis to be sure I understood you correctly.") Copy relevant decision makers on progress report emails in order to maintain transparency and gain direction and support.

SHOW-OFFS

Show-Offs are conceited and aloof bosses, ostentatious about their achievements.

Show-Offs want to impress you. Instead of interrupting you, they snub you. These bosses are snooty and snobbishly superior. Being high-achievers, they consider themselves in the exclusive realm of powerful rulers.

What You're Thinking

Okay, he's smart and maybe he has a right to be conceited. And yes, he does have responsibility for making the tough decisions. But why does he have to make me feel so stupid? He tricks me into giving him inappropriate answers. I get the feeling that he's toying with all of us on his staff to satisfy his insatiable ego.

A Show-Off's Thoughts

My staff people have great potential, of course, or I wouldn't have selected each and every one of them. They have to understand the opportunity for growth that I offer them by working with me. I don't want any surprises from them that could embarrass me. A little intimidation should prevent that. They're going to have to earn my trust. If they're as smart as I think they are, we will get some excellent work done here.

STRATEGY

Keep your eye on your goal. You want to succeed in the organization. You have the chance to learn from a master.

1. *Keep still and observe.* Your confidence grows out of knowing what you do well and working on what you want to improve. You alone determine if you want to keep positive or negative thoughts in your head. No one can make you feel stupid except yourself. So don't get into a bragging contest with a braggart, especially one whose office is decorated in Early Show-Off, with acclamations adorning each inch of wall space.

2. *Deserve your boss's confidence.* Prove yourself by your good performance. Learn the way the boss wants you to process assignments and report progress. Let him know if you anticipate trouble ahead, but don't tell him how to resolve the problem unless he asks for your suggestions.

TACTICAL TALK

You: *From the goals we agreed on, I've prepared this PERT chart in Excel, indicating the objectives for each goal, whom we must contact by what date, and the various approaches we'll use. How does this look to you? I posted it on Google Docs as well, so we can both refer to it easily.*

Or: *Boss, you might want to take a look at these figures. It's possible that a pattern may be developing that could present some difficulty when we try to implement the new method. . . .*

> **Tip:** Make your motto "Listen and learn" when you're working for a clever, conceited Show-Off boss. You needn't bow down in the presence of intellectual royalty, but do remain open and ready to follow his lead.

Whether or not they have earned the right to be exorbitantly proud of themselves, egotistical bosses provide you with opportunities. If, on the one hand, the boss is a pompous airhead, he'll probably be happy for you to leap in and lead the group—provided you are aboveboard and tactful about it. If, on the other hand, your boss is bright, then swallow your pride and absorb whatever you can. This may prove to be one of your best learning experiences.

CHAPTER 17

WHEN YOUR COLLEAGUES ARE SELF-SEEKING

- **One-Uppers**
- **Know-It-Alls**
- **Smashers**

Although you're on the same peer level as your egotistical colleagues, they act as though their jobs are more important than yours. Whatever you're doing, they know more about it than you do.

Whether they are real experts or phony pretenders, you resent their acting as though they are the center of the universe.

More than that, you're upset that they allow their arrogance and conceit to mislead you and deceive you and even humiliate you, in order to make themselves appear more important.

ONE-UPPERS

One-Uppers have to top whatever you say and go you one better.

Braggart colleagues come in two brands—ept and inept. Both types have an extraordinary need for your admiration and choose an irritating way to get you to think they're important.

They blatantly lay claim to a mastery of procedures, sharpened technical skills, friends in high places—anything to impress you with how much they know or who they know. And they don't mind exaggerating to make the point.

What You're Thinking

I am every bit as capable as Abigail. I resent her implication that she can do anything better than I can. Even the last time I was out sick, she bragged she was sicker! She talks with such confidence and overabundance of pride, I wonder if she realizes that she keeps putting me down. She says, "My reports are sharp and crisp" or "My team always exceeds our production goals" in that superconfident tone that implies I don't measure up. She's friendly enough, but I'm sure that's a phony act. I can see right through it.

A One-Upper's Thoughts

I envy the way Elizabeth speaks so effectively before the group. I wish she could see that I can do a lot of things well, too. In fact, I don't know how some of my teammates ever got to this level. They don't belong, but I'll smile and be friendly to them. That's the politically smart way to act.

STRATEGY

To relieve your own stress, you want to bring about a friendlier atmosphere. This will require *mutual* respect and acknowledgment. Stop playing the One-Upper's "I can do anything better than you can" game.

1. *Tease One-Uppers in a light, friendly tone.* Show sensitivity, even though they don't, by gently interrupting the self-aggrandizement

act. If you find yourself tempted to brag back, smile, excuse yourself, and take a seat on the other side of the room.

2. *Give One-Uppers the recognition they've earned.* Find specific areas in which they actually do excel. You'll win their friendship and cooperation by bolstering them with sincere, genuine compliments.

TACTICAL TALK

You: *(Smiling, without sarcasm.) Abigail, here's a glass of water. Your throat must be dry. Take a breather. You've been talking nonstop for the past ten minutes.*

Or: *Look, Abigail, no one can hold a candle to you when it comes to organizing your staff. You've got us all beat with your ability to coordinate. But on this issue we have an additional factor that must be considered. What do you suggest we do about the time limitation?*

Tip: Give One-Uppers the one thing they want most—your attention—and they won't be desperate to point out their great achievements. They feel justified in assuming an arrogant air because they think, in some way, you have belittled their efforts. Consider their expressed conceit a cry for your compliments.

KNOW-IT-ALLS

Know-It-Alls are smart alecks, arrogantly claiming to know everything about everything.

Bursting with self-confidence, Know-It-Alls are obnoxious extroverts who cram their opinions down your throat. Masters at promoting themselves, these colleagues usually know a great deal.

Know-It-Alls flaunt their intelligence, with their vanity shining through every line. Because they are competent, efficient, and thorough planners who cover all the angles, they have little use for your input, and they have no tolerance if you subject their opinionated statements to debate.

What You're Thinking

William appears harmless. He conducts himself with dignity, but I can feel his attitude of superiority. After talking the boss into creating a new program, William lectured the rest of us about achieving company goals by improving our working techniques. I've carefully analyzed my notes and I've concluded a few of the techniques he advocated are potentially dangerous because they violate company policy. I have this tremendous urge to expose the holes in his argument because of his condescending tone.

A Know-It-All's Thoughts

Although I'd never say anything, it's obvious to me that my colleagues can be pretty dense. If the boss doesn't shape them up, I think I should. My talk at the meeting should show them I know all the answers.

STRATEGY

Since Know-It-Alls are usually right, your goal is to extract and utilize the clever thoughts that make them crow, without letting their words stick in your craw.

1. *Listen carefully to formulate good questions.* Don't interrupt with counterarguments but with strong, solid questions. Ask, for example, how this compares, what results have been reported, over what period of time, or what resources are required.

2. *Do your own homework.* Verify the information. If you think Know-It-Alls are wrong, present contradictory data in a matter-of-fact way. Don't directly challenge their expertise, but suggest another way to view the situation.

TACTICAL TALK

You: *How would that affect the rate, and what is the estimated cost for the first year?*

Or: *I know this won't solve our problem, but what if we were to start here instead? Do you think that might give us the impetus we need?*

> **Tip:** Know-It-Alls are bright and usually right. On those occasions you're sure they're wrong, if you try a frontal attack or back them into a corner, Know-It-Alls will bombard you with a ton of irrelevant data to support their position. They consider any opposition a personal affront. The only way to quiet them is to offer them a gracious way to save face.

SMASHERS

Smashers believe that by pushing you down, they elevate themselves.

They deliberately humiliate you in order to become the center of attention. These colleagues feel threatened whenever you do well, because they hold themselves up in comparison to you and feel compelled to attack.

According to their screwed-up value system, if you perform well, that automatically means that their performance is worse than yours. However, work must be judged on its own merit. The value is constant; it doesn't fluctuate by comparison. Your good job can't make another's appear worse (or better) than it actually is. You're not good because someone else is bad. You and they are as good—or as bad—as you always were, independent of each other.

Nevertheless, Smashers, lacking faith in their own abilities, need to push you down so they can feel that they've risen to or above your level.

What You're Thinking

Since the boss assigned Nathan and me to switch jobs, Nathan's been unable to let go. He makes statements to clients that he was better at my new job than I am. He says that I don't belong there, as he did, because I don't have his instincts for meeting client needs.

A Smasher's Thoughts

What is Jerry trying to do, show me up? Well, I'll show him. If I can get them to see how weak Jerry appears, they'll appreciate how strong I really am.

STRATEGY

Your goal is to help Smashers feel confident in their own abilities without using comparisons as a measuring stick.

1. *Acknowledge their expertise.* Give or share credit with Smashers for improving a poor situation. If you let them feel important, they'll feel less need to tear you down. Be extra sensitive about soothing wounded egos. Then, if trouble erupts involving your team, they are more likely to come to you first before running to report it to the boss and others.

2. *Keep abreast of what's happening in the office.* Meet often or have weekly lunches with the Smashers and your other peers. Establish

and maintain good rapport. Discuss ways to cooperate and help each other.

3. *Find little ways to involve your colleagues.* Whether it's taking them into your confidence, asking for advice, requesting a small favor, or asking them to do a small segment of your project in return for your doing something for them, attempt to make them a small part of what you're doing. Now they have a vested interest in your doing well.

TACTICAL TALK

You: *Nathan, I must say, you handled that crisis very smoothly and calmly. If you hadn't, we could have had a real emergency here.*

Or: *The division directors are getting together informally for lunch on Tuesday. I hope you can join us, Nathan, because I think we can help each other solve some mutual problems.*

Or: *Nathan, in the interest of time and efficiency, what would you say to joining forces, with my division doing this part and your division doing that?*

> **Tip:** It's difficult to mold a team when some members are driven by compulsive self-interest. Being terribly impressed with themselves, they not only affect you but also can damage the morale of all subordinates—yours and theirs—with such outbursts as, "Don't you know who I am? I'll have your job!" When Smashers step on you and stomp on your workers, save your sanity by building up their self-confidence.

When the actions and habits of self-centered colleagues interfere with your work, decide it's time to make friends, not enemies. Arguing with the egotistical easily escalates to spitefulness and hatred. Look beyond the conceit and stay calm, for your own good. Note how Thomas Jefferson exercised self-control in this excerpt from his writings: "When I hear another express an opinion which is not mine, I say to myself, he has a right to his opinion as I to mine; why should I question it? His error does me no injury. . . . It is his affair, not mine, if he prefers error."

CHAPTER 18

WHEN YOUR SUBORDINATES ARE SELF-SEEKING

- **Empire Builders**
- **Prima Donnas**
- **Magnifiers**

Egotistical subordinates are preoccupied with their own welfare and advancement. They weigh how some thought or deed will affect their position before they take action. Some demand special consideration because they happen to have important contacts or possess an unusual skill that you desperately need.

If they can't see how it benefits their particular job or project, these self-indulgent workers are unconcerned with the big, broad picture. If they don't perceive an obvious personal gain or advantage, they can become careless in their performance or concentrate only on those parts of the job that will further their goals. When you're trying to supervise and motivate a team, they're a demoralizing influence.

EMPIRE BUILDERS

Empire Builders are climbers. Their interest in others is limited to how well the others serve as stepping-stones.

With one-track minds, egocentric subordinates go about their work as though they are the only ones who count. The view of most of the group is that Empire Builders don't carry their share of the load. They aren't team players but grandstanders who love to hog the limelight and pitch in when they know they'll get attention. They're not motivated by what's good for the group, but by the amount of personal glory an action can generate.

Empire Builders are astute in understanding the political implications of an issue. They've memorized the little boxes on the organizational chart. They know the flow of information and where decisions are made. Doing favors (and, in turn, being owed favors) is their way of amassing a combination of multilevel supporters. Their giant egos and insensitivity enable them to use people as stepping-stones in building their little empires.

What You're Thinking

Kaylee is charming, animated, and persuasive when it serves her purpose. At our staff meetings, she's quick to volunteer and is full of helpful suggestions. I've heard grumbling, though, that when it's time to work on a team project—a joint effort—Kaylee either does a vanishing act or manages to seize control of the group. If she can't milk the activity for personal recognition, she disappears and talks someone else into doing her assignment. On the other hand, if the project has the potential for favorable publicity, she takes over, offering a better way to implement the planning.

An Empire Builder's Thoughts

I think it's important to get the boss to assign me to our division's planning team. From what I read on the company blog, that project is in line with the major emphasis the CEO articulated in his talk to the board. I think I see a way to expand our results beyond our own division, gradually including all the other divisions. That would allow me to work with several key people I might not otherwise have the chance to know, and hopefully win me favorable attention from the higher-ups.

STRATEGY

Your goal is to walk a tightrope. Maintain the Empire Builders' enthusiasm and effectiveness while preventing them from dumping on fellow workers in order to promote themselves.

1. *Applaud the Empire Builders' talent for exciting the crowd.* Use the Empire Builders' strengths to generate enthusiasm for a new initiative or direction.
2. *Set a limit on the Empire Builders' behavior.* Decide exactly what you won't tolerate. You can't change the Empire Builders' personalities, but you can change the way you interact with them.

TACTICAL TALK

You: *Kaylee, you have such a great organizing skill, I'd like you to set up a contest by devising four planning teams for our division, each to explore fresh ways to achieve our objectives.*

Or: *Kaylee, explain to me why you felt you had to have Wayne take over for you while you attended that departmental meeting. . . . Wayne's already carrying a heavy load, and adding anything more is a* *serious imposition. From now on, if you want to change assign-ments, see me first.*

> **Tip:** Empire Builder subordinates are both a help and a hindrance. Encourage them to lead, but insist on their adherence to your rules. Apply a "latitude with limits" approach when managing an Empire Builder.

PRIMA DONNAS

Prima Donnas are self-entitled, temperamental workers, demanding that you give them special treatment.

Often conceited and vain performers, Prima Donnas have a way of intimidating and manipulating you into believing the company will fold without them. We can speculate that they were spoiled as children and learned early how to get others to do their work for them. They aren't lazy, but shrewd.

They use many tricks, such as issuing ultimatums, to get special attention. In return for certain demands, they dangle prizes you long for, such as promising to introduce you to decision makers who can close a deal. Generally, Prima Donnas are moody and have short fuses. The danger is that they wear down your resistance and are detrimental to the team.

What You're Thinking

Most of my staff gladly cooperate when I make assignments, but I can count on Wyatt to give me a hard time. There's always some special circumstance why he can't work late or on the weekend or head the project.

He gets upset when he's faced with doing something he obviously doesn't want to do. Rather than start a scene, I've been giving in to his temperamental antics. Wyatt is driving me crazy because he makes it so difficult for me to treat each subordinate impartially.

A Prima Donna's Thoughts

I've given this company plenty of my time and energy. I don't see any reason to take on any extra work. The others may fall for that line about all of us having to pitch in to reduce the caseload. Well, let the peasants perform. I'm going to get out of it because the boss is afraid to antagonize me.

STRATEGY

Your objective is to maintain control by guiding the Prima Donnas to act more responsibly.

1. *Call their bluff.* Stop acting intimidated and allowing Prima Donnas to interfere with your operation. Whatever Prima Donnas have that you want, it's better to do without it than to have them usurp your authority and destroy team morale.
2. *Help them take ownership of their role within the team.* Be friendly, but very firm, in insisting that your procedures be followed. Remind them that everyone is needed to meet the aggressive deadline. Enlist the support of the Prima Donnas' peers to apply pressure on them to join in.

TACTICAL TALK

You: *Well, Wyatt, I'm afraid you're going to have to change that appointment. I need you to take these cases. That's the only fair way to distribute them. Thank you for understanding the situation.*

Or: *Wyatt, the management team has come up with a plan to reduce the caseload. It involves you, Jodi, George, and Alex because we consider you the strongest workers. You'll form a task force that would take only those cases that . . .*

> **Tip:** Recognize the games that Prima Donnas play. Like children who pout, stomp their feet, and throw tantrums, they use a variety of irritating techniques to wear you down and get their own way. You have to reinforce your rules and stick to them.

MAGNIFIERS

Magnifiers blow minor tasks out of proportion to make themselves appear more important.

Magnifiers enlarge *whatever* they do, making even the insignificant a very big deal. They are immature in their desire to impress others with unimportant work; although, admittedly, the busywork may be well executed.

Magnifiers often complain they haven't time for their important assignments. They're too busy attempting to get noticed by giving each little job all they've got, whether or not it deserves the effort. These subordinates have to grow up emotionally.

What You're Thinking

Jasmine spends far too much time designing fancy charts that we really don't need. I guess I've been too subtle with her. I'm going to have to clamp down about priority items. Also, for someone so new to the job, she certainly presumed to have all the answers. Jasmine was determined to call attention to herself before gaining any experience in this position when she volunteered an article for the company blog. Imagine telling everyone how our services could be improved, only to learn a little later that many of her conclusions are unworkable at this company. Her determination to make her job bigger than it is embarrasses me and the rest of my team.

A Magnifier's Thoughts

I want them all to see that this new kid on the block is going to make a big difference to the company. I've done my research, tracing the routes of our various systems. I've also prepared a series of charts breaking down all the information. I know the boss will understand that I haven't had time to get to some of the things he asked me to do, but I'm sure he'll be pleasantly surprised to see what a grand job I've done in compiling this data.

STRATEGY

Your goal is to help Magnifiers distinguish between assignments that are top priority and those to be dispatched quickly with minimum effort.

1. *Differentiate between important tasks and busywork.* Explain that one should feel justifiable pride for achieving high standards where it is warranted, and no pride for wasting time on the unimportant. Until they learn the difference, avoid giving Magnifiers assignments that must be handled immediately.
2. *Develop a rating code and deadlines.* For example, use simple A, B, and C categories to indicate the time and effort required for different tasks. Make it clear that their designated tasks must be completed by the deadline date before working on anything else.

You: *Jasmine, you are capable of fine work, and in time you will be recognized for meeting the high standards of this department. But first you have to stop enlarging minor tasks to make them appear greater than they really are, and concentrate on completing your assignments.*

Or: *I'm confident you will do well here once you learn to follow a few simple procedures.*

> **Tip:** Magnifiers insist on overstating and overemphasizing every little task they perform, to try to increase your perception of their importance. Such behavior indicates emotional immaturity and requires your firm hand.

As the manager, you're charged with building a strong and effective team. Regardless of the value of their contributions, you can't allow any self-centered subordinates to dictate to you what, how, when, and if they will do what you ask. You can show sensitive concern for individuals and sincere appreciation for their efforts and still maintain necessary discipline with fair and impartial treatment for all.

PART SEVEN

Dealing with Procrastinating or Vacillating People

People who *irrationally* postpone what they have to do generally have vulnerable self-esteem. Although others may praise and encourage them, these bosses, colleagues, and subordinates doubt themselves and keep putting off making decisions and taking action. Just one critical comment can result in another delay.

The delays affect the entire operation. Procrastinators and vacillators cause last-minute scurrying accompanied by tension and arguments. Decisions and output are not quite as good as they might have been if it all hadn't been so rush-rush.

Procrastinators frequently blame their habit of putting things off on not having enough time. Of course, they have the same number of hours as everyone else; but they may try to do too much at once or fritter away their time on the insignificant. The stalling is not rooted in a time shortage, but in fear or rebellion. Some fear that what they do or say won't meet their excessively high standards, or fear they can't do the deed correctly. Rebel-stallers find that holding up the whole office gives them a measure of control over the bosses or colleagues they want to avenge.

CHAPTER 19

WHEN YOUR BOSS CAUSES DELAYS

- **Put-Offs**
- **Helter-Skelters**
- **Overcommitters**
- **Chameleons**

The whole organization is thrown off-kilter when the procrastinating or vacillating attitude starts at the top and runs downhill. Some bosses stall until they get up their nerve to act. They lack a leader's confidence.

Some bosses change their minds because they never wanted to make the move in the first place. They start out with a pleasant teasing of "We'll see" and eventually agree only to avoid an argument. Others seesaw between yes and no as easily as a chameleon changes its colors.

While problems facing procrastinating and vacillating bosses vary, your direction in dealing with them is clear: You have to move them—and yourself—out of the stuck position.

PUT-OFFS

Put-Offs are decision makers who drag their feet but get back to you eventually.

While stallers hope the issue will go away, Put-Offs appear to agree with you. Your concern is simply not their priority. Their evasive language is deceiving. You become increasingly frustrated, unable to understand why they delay. It's like pulling teeth to get a firm commitment.

This problem is frustrating in the typical boss-worker relationship that occurs within the four walls of an office building. Remote workers and independent contractors also have to deal with decision makers who put them on hold. They've invested so much time, they don't know what else they can do to push things along. Should they give up and cut their losses? Not yet. There are still a few things to try.

What You're Thinking

That proposal I submitted was top-notch. I could sense that Dawn was quite receptive. She saw the potential when I gave my presentation, and she's the one who gives the final okay. Also, there was no serious objection from the committee that considers and recommends proposals. Although Dawn has told me a few times that we'll soon have a meeting, she still hasn't agreed to one. What's holding her up? What would impel a favorable decision? I need some kind of answer. If this doesn't work out, I'll have to start considering alternatives.

A Put-Off's Thoughts

Noah keeps asking for a meeting to discuss that proposal. I think it has considerable promise, although I could suggest a few important changes. However, my time is already so overcommitted that I don't know when I can squeeze that in. Noah is so enthusiastic, I hate to hurt his feelings. I'll just keep putting him off until I have more time to deal with this decision.

STRATEGY

Your objective is to get a decision very soon and, hopefully, in your favor.

1. *Stop pushing.* Lower your level of enthusiasm. Don't expose your impatience or annoyance at the indecision. To counteract the guilt many Put-Offs feel about disappointing you, convey your desire to improve. Show you welcome their suggestions.

2. *Make it easy for Put-Offs to level with you.* Then you can help them deal painlessly with the real reason behind the stall. Gently probe with indirect questions. Aid in clarifying and prioritizing goals and objectives so that you both get a better understanding of what's required. Suggest alternatives.

3. *Pick up on evasive terminology.* Listen especially for qualifying words that hint at what's causing the delay. Keep eye contact, listen to the speaker, and don't interrupt. Concentrate on what isn't said—facial expressions, gestures, tone, and tempo.

4. *Tap into their most compelling desire.* Go beyond what they need or want; search for what they long for and tie this to your proposal. Show that your main concern is for them rather than for yourself because you, uniquely, have just what they're looking for.

TACTICAL TALK

Dawn: *Noah, I'm sorry but I just haven't had the chance to look at the proposal more closely. I'll have to meet with you in a couple of weeks, after I get a lot of important stuff out of the way.*

You: *I understand. (Graciously letting her off the hook.) However, I would like to leave you with this thought. I see my role as making you the most recognized CEO in the industry. (Her longing is your lure.)*

Dawn: *(She can't resist wanting to hear more.) Wow! That's quite ambitious.*

You: *But entirely possible if you could spare just a couple of minutes now to tell me your initial reaction to the presentation.*

Dawn: *I thought it was rather promising. (Her use of "rather" indicates she's hinting it needs improvement.)*

You: *Of course, even good proposals can be made better.*

Dawn: *It was good, but not exactly what we want.*

You: *Okay, what objectives are we trying to get closer to?*

Dawn: *Well, I wonder if this could be a little more hard-hitting? And the examples need more universal appeal.*

You: *That's certainly doable. I've been studying the trends and researching the data. I know how to add the punch you're looking for. If I email the changes to you tomorrow morning, can you see me for a few minutes at 5 PM?*

Dawn: *All right. I'll see you then.*

Tip: Listen closely to catch the hints that Put-Offs give you. Chances are they want to be straightforward with you but won't speak directly for fear that you can't take criticism and they'll hurt your feelings.

HELTER-SKELTERS

Helter-Skelters are bosses who have great difficulty meeting deadlines because of their flimsy, unstructured methods.

Everyone has to scramble at the last minute to meet agreements. There's one crisis after another. Without clearly defining who's to do what by when, these bosses cause the office to be plagued with confusion.

While people often complain about bosses who are mean, just as troublesome are managers who are too nice—so nice that they're reluctant to issue orders. It's difficult to tell pleasant, friendly managers that their unsystematic methods are resulting in problems. But if you don't want to be exhausted by putting out daily fires, that's what you have to do—tactfully and professionally.

What You're Thinking

We miss or nearly miss deadlines because of the boss's disorderly methods. And, with no definite accountability, there's a constant last-minute rush to meet the promised times. She seems to have difficulty telling us what to do and adjusting priorities to avoid emergencies. I hate to hurt her feelings, but we definitely need some clear directives and delegation of responsibilities.

A Helter-Skelter's Thoughts

I believe I've created a fine, friendly team environment in this office. I can still remember supervisors who were always barking orders and making everyone tense. Here, everyone is happy to pitch in, despite the interruptions and distractions. I trust my people to come through for us.

STRATEGY

This is no horse race; you have to remove the boss's blinders.

1. *Prepare a time sheet.* As an opener, show how long it's been taking to handle crises. You can then discuss how these could be managed faster.

2. *Suggest project management software.* Explain that this allows you to see the status of projects and when they're due. Suggest using a tool like Google Docs to encourage collaboration and accountability.

3. *Prepare charts for bosses who need hard-copy reminders.* After the desired result is identified with a Gantt chart, approximate the time for each step and note to whom the work is assigned, all arranged in logical sequence with a realistic schedule. Or show a PERT chart. With vertical columns for weeks or months, break down assignments into critical subgoals by drawing a horizontal start-to-finish dateline for each specific task. Send updated charts regularly by email and post them in Google Docs.

4. *Request brief, regular weekly staff meetings.* Meeting for just fifteen minutes will help everybody stay focused on goals and priorities, check progress, make adjustments, and delegate decision making to avoid deadline emergencies. For virtual teams and remote workers, regular weekly videoconferences can do the trick.

TACTICAL TALK

You: *Boss, I know how hard you've tried to create an easygoing atmosphere, and all of us appreciate that. However, there's something I feel you'd want me to call to your attention. We seem to be expending a lot of time that's cutting into our productivity and profit. Take a look at this time sheet.*

Boss: *Oh, I had no idea this—*

You: *(Interrupting, to put a positive slant.) I'd like to show you a couple of things I think could help us. (Using "us" says we're part of a team. Explain the software and the charts.)*

Boss: *Well, I suppose we could be more definite about the assignments. Why don't we work on these tomorrow morning? You've given me a lot to think about.*

You: *I'd be glad to help. I know how important it is to you that we all get along. Maybe if the staff could meet each week for just a few minutes, we can clear up potential problems.*

Boss: *That's not a bad idea.*

Tip: No matter the reason your manager fails to manage, you can step up to the plate. Politely manage your manager. As long as you are careful and respectful, you can guide the operation and eliminate most of the emergencies.

OVERCOMMITTERS

Overcommitters are nice people who can't refuse anyone and then find they have no time to follow through.

You can count on Overcommitters to love harmony. These bosses agree with whatever anyone asks of them, because they hate to argue. A confrontation could hurt someone's feelings and therefore has to be avoided.

But by *pretending* to agree in order to prevent a fight or a fuss, Overcommitters promise too much or promise to do something they don't really agree with. Overburdened and unable to handle it all, they put off action or decisions and break their promises. They don't mean any harm, but you certainly resent the way they've messed up your timetable and failed to come through with whatever you were depending on.

What You're Thinking

Promises, promises, my boss keeps breaking promises. I end up looking foolish because I had reassured my staff that the boss would have an answer for us today regarding the holiday schedule. She's always disappointing us. All that agreeableness is a phony facade, and "We're all one big happy family" is just a line. I'm losing respect for her. What's worse, how can I ever trust what she says she's going to do?

An Overcommitter's Thoughts

I'd like to agree to the team's request, granting permission for them to leave a few hours early on Friday before the start of the holidays. But I'm concerned about getting out the quarterlies on time. Maybe we'll need those extra hours to finish up. I know I promised them an answer today, but I'm going to have to give this more thought. What can I do to keep the team from getting upset?

STRATEGY

Your goal is to help your boss make decisions without feeling threatened by unpopularity.

1. *Claim the problem as your own.* When you sense the boss is stuck on the horns of a dilemma ("Should I please the company or please my workers?"), remove one of the horns so that the boss no longer has to choose. Step forward and accept the problem as *your* responsibility.
2. *Bring the priorities into focus.* Assist in finding ways for the boss to do the right thing. It's possible to carry out a manager's responsibility to the organization and, at the same time, lessen the anticipated negative impact upon subordinates. Study the situation, examine everyone's needs, and then offer potential solutions. You can probably negotiate a win-win compromise.

TACTICAL TALK

You: *Boss, I've been thinking that the request we made for extra hours off on Friday might have put you in an awkward position. How about* *my kicking around some ideas with my staff on how this could be managed and still stick to our original schedule?*

Or: *Boss, my staff suggests that they can finish the quarterlies by working late on Thursday, substituting those extra hours for time off Friday afternoon. Is that okay with you?*

Tip: Overcommitter bosses create dilemmas for themselves when they take their eyes off their priorities and become overly concerned with pleasing the immediate world. You can best move them to action either by removing one side of the dilemma or by offering additional options that allow the boss to escape through the dilemma's horns.

CHAMELEONS

Chameleons are changeable and indecisive, and they waver on their decisions.

While Overcommitters break promises in the name of harmony, Chameleons go back on their word because of their insecurity. Sometimes Chameleon bosses are incompetent. They may have been promoted beyond their capabilities. Rather than admit they don't know what they're doing, they delay deciding what to do. They say one thing today and the opposite tomorrow, deliberately muddying the waters.

Sometimes Chameleons are looking for the absolutely perfect decision. They think they've found it, then discover a flaw in the chosen option and change their minds again.

Wishy-washy and inconsistent, Chameleons sway back and forth. Organized types (who plan for every contingency except individual idiosyncrasies) find it particularly infuriating when they believe the boss has settled an issue, only to find it wasn't settled at all.

What You're Thinking

I'm supposed to be my boss's right-hand man, but I'm finding it very difficult to help him. It seems to me that he's unsure of himself. He doesn't know whether he's doing the right thing, so he waffles on his directives. The Fenton deal was typical. Last week he wanted to proceed with the contract full steam ahead. This week he tells me to cancel our meetings and stop the negotiations. It's impossible to get anything accomplished when bosses keep changing their minds.

A Chameleon's Thoughts

I thought when I took this job it would be an easy transition. After all, everyone knows that managerial skills are transferable. The problem is, without knowing the history and politics of this division, I really have to be terribly careful not to make a horrendously costly error. Right now, I'm not sure which staff people I can trust.

STRATEGY

Your goal is to expedite decisions so that issues that have been left hanging can finally be resolved. This requires your making a special effort to earn the boss's confidence.

1. *Refine the content of information.* Even if the boss isn't new to this job, fill him in on essential background data. But don't give your boss more information about a subject than he needs to know in order to decide. Analyze, then summarize. Offer the boss suggested solutions instead of just dumping problems.

2. *Negotiate the level of information.* Does the boss really have to make *all* those decisions? Can he delegate responsibility to you for signing off on specified types of actions? In your discussions, maintain a calm manner in order to be more persuasive.

3. *Monitor the flow of information.* Keep close track of due dates for deliverables. Set reminders on Outlook or on your smartphone to flag your attention, well in advance of deadlines, about the status of your projects. If you don't wait until the last minute to check progress, you can usually avoid gridlock.

TACTICAL TALK

You: *(Instead of "What should we do about . . . ?") Boss, as you know, we're looking at three alternatives: 1) . . . , 2) . . . , and 3). . . . It seems that the second option is best for us at this time because . . . Does it strike you the same way?*

Or: *Boss, as you know, I've been working on this for several years. Wouldn't it help ease some of your burden if I okayed the first two steps and you gave final approval on the last three?*

> **Tip:** Bosses who vacillate can be bolstered by receiving clear, concise, pertinent information. They're not supposed to be experts on everything. Recognize the areas where your boss needs additional support. Supply the vital information in a form that can be immediately utilized, and you'll earn your boss's trust.

You're not your boss's keeper. How bosses choose to act is their own responsibility, so don't complain about the delays they cause or make excuses for them. Your aim is to help facilitate the operational flow. Your boss may have been selected to head your project because he or she has certain talents that aren't obvious to you. When bosses cause delays, you can assume they're probably afraid of failing or feel threatened. You can help by supplying them with whatever data is needed to make good, solid, final decisions.

CHAPTER 20

WHEN YOUR COLLEAGUES CAUSE DELAYS

- **Socializers**
- **Perfectionists**
- **Dawdlers**

Like their bosses, your colleagues' delaying tactics may also be rooted in fear of failure, but there's another component. Generally, peer procrastinators are so wrapped up in pursuing their own objectives, interests, or pleasures that they don't realize how their actions are affecting the entire office.

Some are too busy being friendly, others are too concerned with their own image, and some are too careless about deadlines to meet their responsibilities.

SOCIALIZERS

Socializers put off work while they chat with colleagues, post on social media, and "play" online.

These socializing peers who are dedicated to having fun don't seem to take anything seriously. In their pursuit of happiness, they overstep the line between friendliness and responsibility, accenting the former and ignoring the latter. Socializer colleagues are outgoing and truly want to count everyone as a friend.

They stop by your desk for a long exchange. They get the group together for lunch. They're always texting or taking a coffee break. They have time for everything except the finished product they promised you. Maybe the work is too difficult for them. Maybe they're afraid they'll get it wrong. Maybe they disapprove of the system. Whatever is making them procrastinate, one thing we do know: They certainly find it more pleasant to be doing something other than the assigned task.

Socializers are happy, friendly people, and you enjoy their company. But they interrupt everyone else's routine and cause serious delays. You find yourself becoming increasingly agitated by their antics.

What You're Thinking

Molly is a great person, with a big heart, and lots of fun. But she reminds me of the kid who won't stop playing long enough to do her homework. It's not my place to lecture her. I just wish I had a magic wand that could get her to settle down and do her work. I can't move on this project until Molly gives me her estimates.

A Socializer's Thoughts

I really enjoy working here. This is such a pleasant office, and I've made a lot of good friends. Which reminds me, I have to call the gang to see if we can meet for lunch today, and if we're going to get that softball team organized. . . .

STRATEGY

Although you have no authority over them, your goal is to persuade the Socializers to cooperate and finish their assignments.

1. *Spell out the importance of the task and the roles they play.* Let Socializers know the benefits to the company, department, and workers if the assignment is done well—and the consequences if it is not. Impress upon them that they control an essential factor in making it happen. Be sincere; no phony lines.

2. *Limit your request to your immediate concern.* Don't ask for anything except the exact piece of work you need from them at this moment. Keep the focus and the discussion on that one item. Build grace periods into your original planning (for example, setting deadlines for their work the week before you actually need it) to allow for their delaying tactics.

3. *Push politely without revealing panic.* Control your temper and hide your annoyance. Be pleasant about asking for what you have to have, but don't apologize for interrupting them. Act friendly and self-assured to win their confidence.

4. *Ask them for their opinions.* Help them to feel more involved, that they are truly a part of what is going on. You may hear ideas for changes that could unblock a logjam or even improve results.

5. *Tie together what you want with their particular longing or interest.* As you chat, you'll hear Socializers express their desires ("I wish I could . . . ," "I wish that I had . . ."). Try to see a situation the way they see it, and suggest that finishing the task will help them achieve that desire.

TACTICAL TALK

You: *Frankly, Molly, I know you're a fair person and you want to do your part. The fact is, we're stuck because you are the only one who knows how to figure these kinds of estimates. What we need right now is just that one figure.*

Or: *Do you have any ideas on why we get so jammed up? What do you think we might try to move things a little faster?*

Or: *This will call for a celebration when we finish, and you're our resident expert in how to have fun.*

> **Tip:** Socializers missed their calling. They'd be great recreation directors. To win their cooperation, first win their trust by leveling with them. Don't plead for yourself, but press for them to do what is important for themselves and for the company. Then link that effort to whatever it is they hanker for.

PERFECTIONISTS

Perfectionists keep polishing their work, but it never meets their extravagant standards.

These colleagues expect too much from themselves. They think everything they attempt should meet their excessively high expectations. As smart as they usually are, Perfectionists are consummate worriers.

They're afraid the work won't come up to the ideal they have in their minds, or that they may not get it perfect on their first try. If their workload prohibits their spending extra time to hone, and hone, and hone some more, they feel frustrated. So they keep putting off finishing the assignment. The more they worry, the less they produce. If they don't turn the work in, nobody will know it hasn't reached this artificial, idealized goal they've created in their minds.

What You're Thinking

I don't know what to do with Larry! As our multimedia specialist, if he doesn't come through, I'm going to be in real trouble. I have to make the presentation to our new client on Thursday. So far, all I've seen is his original outline for the video part of the presentation. He says it's almost finished, but he needs to fine-tune it with a little more editing. I'm nervous because Larry is never satisfied with what he produces. What do I do if he doesn't have it ready on time? I can't keep running to the boss to make Larry speed up. I wish I could make Larry understand what's at stake here.

A Perfectionist's Thoughts

I really thought this video for the new client was going to be great. It could be if people would leave me alone and let me smooth all the rough edges. I can't hand it in now. I need more time. I wish everybody would stop bugging me to turn over my work before I'm ready. Maybe the rest of them are satisfied with a less than excellent performance, but I'm not. When my name is on something, it has to represent the very best of my ability. I would be humiliated about turning in anything less than that.

STRATEGY

Your objective is to help Perfectionist colleagues focus on what's important to the company as well as to themselves, and to dovetail their priorities with company goals.

1. *Help Perfectionists deal with reality.* Organizations are limited in the amount of funds allocated and the time and staff assigned to certain projects. This is a hard lesson for all good workers to swallow, but Perfectionists choke on the limitations. If the company can't afford a standard as high as one wants, this shouldn't diminish the worker's self-esteem.

2. *Reassure them that not everything has to be perfect.* Some projects have to be done posthaste, or an opportunity will be lost forever. Then the priority shifts from doing an excellent job at a normal pace to doing a good job quickly. If workers don't produce gems with every try, it doesn't mean they're failures. Therefore, at times it's not only all right to turn in certain things that can't match expectations, it's expected.

3. *Help them with time management.* Suggest that work can be broken down into smaller steps or stages. Perfectionists need to enjoy a sense of accomplishment, which they can get from checking more (and less complicated) completed tasks off their list. Explain that they'll have more time for important projects if they shorten the time spent on the less significant ones.

TACTICAL TALK

You: *Larry, would you like to talk to me about the video part of Thursday's presentation? Is there something in particular that bothers you about it? Maybe if we worked together we'd get the basics done for now, and if that's not up to your standard, you could polish it more for future, more elaborate, presentations.*

Or: *Larry, I know how difficult it is to turn in work that's less than your best when you aren't given enough time. You know the saying, "There's never time to do it right, there's always time to do it over." But the fact is, some projects are pegged as giving little return for effort invested, so the manager scales back the resources going into them. We have to distinguish between these and the projects that allow us to shine. If it's any consolation, even people who are in business for themselves sometimes have to be satisfied with less than the ideal.*

> **Tip:** Don't confuse delaying Perfectionists with closet Perfectionists who, in a highly competitive climate, sneak their work home to enjoy the polishing process on their own time. Without the right encouragement from superiors, they may suffer from stress, but they pose no problem to you because they produce on time. Delaying Perfectionists, on the other hand, throw the rest of you off schedule. To move them more in sync with you and your peers, they need to feel they're part of the team. So talk about team effort and team competition, and plan some team reward or celebration upon project completion.

DAWDLERS

Dawdlers waste time while you wait for their work in order to complete your own.

Dawdlers are late for work, late for meetings, and late for appointments. They may feel insecure about their abilities and try to forestall the results by being late. Their problem becomes your problem when they put off getting you the information you need, signing orders you request, or completing their reports. Worst, they let you cool your heels while awaiting their late arrival.

Wasting time over trifling matters, they loiter and linger. Dawdlers often sit on the fence because they can't reach decisions. It's better, they tell themselves, to gather *all* the facts and hear from everyone before starting. Or they may move from one task to another, never completing anything.

What You're Thinking

This is the third time in a month that Addison has held us up because she didn't process the requisitions that have been sitting on her desk! I don't think she's lazy, but she seems to get distracted easily. Also, it seems to me that she goes through an unusual amount of checking before she okays an order. I suspect she's either not well organized or she's unsure of herself, or both. Still, if I cover for her again, *I'm* the one who will appear incompetent.

A Dawdler's Thoughts

I know I was late processing Megan's requisitions, and she's annoyed with me. But with the last warning I got from the boss, I just can't afford to make another mistake. Actually, the crux of the problem is old software and systems. With a new computer program, I could stay on top of all those orders with a quick update of current price lists. However, it's clear that nobody wants my opinion. They just want to yell at me for being unreliable.

STRATEGY

Your goal is to free yourself from your colleagues' apparently irresponsible behavior. If you can also direct Dawdlers toward improvement, that's a bonus for all of you.

1. *Ask for clarification of responsibilities.* Request that your boss review deadlines and workflow patterns with the whole staff. The responsibility for handling nonperformance by fellow workers is with the boss, the appointing authority. If you keep covering up for Dawdlers, the real core of the problem can never be uprooted.

2. *Help Dawdlers get organized without criticizing them.* For assignments on which you are jointly involved, agree in advance on a reasonable amount of time needed. Discuss potential obstacles and how they can be met or skirted. Together, produce your task and deadline plans.

3. *Teach Dawdlers to be punctual.* Start without them, rather them hold up a group meeting for the chronically tardy. Plan appointments with them in *your* office. Their being late won't bother you so much if you can continue working until they show up. Tell them an earlier time than you actually expect to start. Don't throw your other appointments off because of Dawdlers. If their being late means you can't finish with them, stop at the allotted time and reschedule.

TACTICAL TALK

You: *Addison, I can't keep covering for you. From now on, if you can't get your work done on time, you'll have to handle the problem yourself. There's something wrong here that you'll have to settle with the boss.*

Or: *Boss, I think it would help us all if we could develop a flowchart, setting forth our deadlines and showing how our individual roles in this project meld.*

Or: *Andy, please tell Addison I couldn't wait any longer. I have to leave now or I'll be late for another appointment.*

Or: *Boss, Addison and I agreed on deadlines to avoid future holdups with items I ordered. Our plan is not working out. I need your help.*

> **Tip:** First distinguish between the two basic classes of colleague Dawdlers—those who are late because of some fault within the system, and those who are habitually late with everything. The former need your help in suggesting procedural revisions. The latter's irresponsible actions should be dealt with by their supervisors. In either case, you're not helping your peers by covering up their bad habits or the organization's bad system.

Procrastinating and vacillating colleagues cause their coworkers unnecessary stress and strain. Quite often, some quirk in their personalities prevents them from following through with their responsibilities. They pursue their own objectives, failing to see the connection between helping the company and helping themselves. Since you have no authority over your peers, if your attempts at personal persuasion don't work, you have to let the boss handle their nonperformance. Sometimes, however, the reason for the delay is a fault within the system, and the procrastinators aren't really offenders but victims. In that case, suggesting revisions to the system could prove most useful.

CHAPTER 21

WHEN YOUR SUBORDINATES CAUSE DELAYS

- **Checklist for Dealing with Procrastinators**
- **Clock-Watchers**
- **Duds**
- **Rebels**

Subordinates who seem bored, scared, or resentful and who dilly-dally instead of doing what they know has to be done create conflict among other workers. Untreated, the tension can grow into a serious loss in productivity.

But before looking at three common types who cause delays—those who won't do, those who can't do, and those seeking revenge—you should carefully examine the climate in your office. If the air engulfing procrastinating subordinates is too stressful, rigid, or frigid, some part of the problem is not with the people but with the system. And sometimes a simple, personal thank-you note changes an attitude.

CHECKLIST FOR DEALING WITH PROCRASTINATORS

Do you create good rapport?

❏ Do you promote a fun, engaging work environment?

❏ Do you establish a good emotional climate in which workers are challenged to learn and produce, and have time to think about trying innovative approaches?

❏ Do you put procrastinators at ease, sensing that you identify with their needs?

❏ Is your office a pleasant and friendly place?

❏ Do you avoid humiliating workers publicly or clobbering them privately after each mistake, allowing them to save face?

❏ Do you "sandwich" negative criticism in between positive, specific praise?

❏ Do you reinforce the procrastinators' identity with their group through informal office get-togethers, events, and friendly competition?

Do you eliminate contributory factors?

❏ Do you check that external factors don't contribute to delays: disturbing noises; poor parking, lighting, and ventilation; wrong tools; malfunctioning equipment; and insufficient training?

❏ Do you have enough staff so that you're not expecting one person to supervise too many workers?

❏ Are you certain your rules aren't wrapped in red tape, overlapping or requiring endless steps to get permission to carry out tasks?

❏ Do you make the objectives, directions, and time frames absolutely clear?

❏ Do you firmly enforce the deadlines you've set and make clear the consequences of nonperformance?

Do you take the time to motivate?

❏ Do you act as though they've already developed a potential capability you've noticed?

❏ Do you set standards, explaining how their jobs contribute to the total effort and what's expected of them, and together prepare a list of responsibilities?

❏ Do you reassure them of your confidence that they can perform well, and do you deliver honest praise when they do?

❏ Do you discover your workers' ego needs and help them feel important, tying training to personal ambition as well as to the actual job problem?

❏ Do you keep your workers informed?

Have you instituted helpful mechanisms and systems?

❏ Do you provide adequate training?

❏ Do you have a plan in place that allows subordinates' ideas to bubble up to the top?

❏ Do you tie incentives to performance, celebrating real accomplishments such as topping a previous record or introducing a new system?

❏ Do you show workers how to break up their jobs into logical parts?

❏ Have you designed a system to reward completion of major stages of a project?

❏ Do you display charts to graphically show status, improvement, and comparison of results among units?

❏ Do you have a system for rewarding workers with recognition events, additional training, raises, and promotions?

CLOCK-WATCHERS

Clock-Watchers try to get away without working. Their attitude says, "It's not my job."

These subordinates look lazy and unconcerned. They resemble

deadwood, shirking work and playing hooky from meetings and projects. Clock-Watchers are capable but refuse to put forth a drop more effort than they have to.

Frequently, their indifference stems from a lack of pride in the company's product or service, or in their particular part in producing it. They see no relationship between their job and the company goals. Nobody ever told them that what they do is important or appreciated.

Sometimes, when you scratch below the apathetic surface, you find subordinates who are frustrated by red tape or a specialty rut. If they're bored, unchallenged, and underutilized, they may deliberately delay turning in their work just to get a little excitement going. They may use procrastination to create problems so that they can be recognized for solving them.

What You're Thinking

I don't know what happened to Lydia. When she first came here, she was so full of promise and excited about working in this company. Now I can't seem to break her what's-the-use attitude. The more I talk, the slower she works. Because we have to process so much data on a daily basis, when Lydia doesn't finish, I have to give the remainder of her work to the faster workers who, of course, resent the overload. They feel they're being punished for working faster. All this has given me one big morale problem.

A Clock-Watcher's Thoughts

When I first came to this office, the boss said they were looking for people able to implement the projects that would move us ahead. I wish I had taped that conversation to play back to him! I am so bored that it's torture to turn out my assigned work. My talent is untapped. I have no chance to contribute, even though I'm sure many times I know a better method than the one they're using. The only way to get any notice around here is to be late with an assignment.

STRATEGY

Your goal is to get Clock-Watchers to assume responsibility for performing their assignments on time, enabling you to treat all your workers fairly and distribute equitable workloads.

1. *Look first at your instructions.* What's crystal clear to you can be blurred confusion to your subordinates. Be sure you've spelled out specific objectives and deadlines.

2. *Ask what's wrong instead of accusing.* Give Clock-Watchers the chance to talk. Ask for their opinions and suggestions, and say that you'll consider them. That doesn't mean you'll use their ideas, but that you will *think* about using them.

3. *Begin a program of pride in the company, department, or job.* Implement a comprehensive approach including individual involvement, such as discussion groups or quality circles, team competition, recognition system, and better channeling of internal and external communications. Seek subordinates' ideas and empower them to make some of the decisions affecting the outcome of their tasks.

4. *Create challenge, excitement, and fun.* To make room for the spontaneous, eliminate extraneous regulations that tie workers down. Utilize their untapped potential. Not using their potential wastes a valuable resource and can be a root cause of worker dissatisfaction. Let subordinates learn something new by attending workshops, seminars, conferences, and training programs.

You: *Frankly, Lydia, I was annoyed that you didn't finish this on time, until it occurred to me that I may not have made clear to you the importance of this deadline.*

Or: *Why do you think you're having trouble completing your assignments? Are there some obstacles you want to talk about? What would you say will happen if you continue . . . ? Can you suggest something we can do to get you back on track?*

Or: *I sense that some of you are getting a little bored, so I'd like all of you to discuss and recommend new ways to make your efforts more satisfying. An example is rotating jobs so that each of you could learn the major aspects of the operation.*

Tip: Don't nag. Learn why procrastinators drag behind. Many Clock-Watchers aspire to go higher. They're competent enough but are frustrated because they are hog-tied or unchallenged. They feel stuck in a job that doesn't fit their ambitions and needs. If you're considering a development program for them, be sure other workers don't perceive this as a reward (as in "I work fast and get loaded down with his unfinished work. He works slowly and gets more training!"). Plan learning opportunities and job rotation as part of the broad picture, after getting input from the entire staff.

DUDS

Duds cause delays because they don't do, or have to redo, their work.

Projects are held up repeatedly when Duds screw up and don't come through. Sometimes the lack of performance is rooted in fear. They may be mismatched for their jobs. They don't know how to do the job and are too embarrassed or afraid to ask for help. Maybe they'll do it wrong, so they're constantly delaying, trying to find the answer themselves.

At other times, the reason is casual indifference. It can be contrasting attitudes between generations that prevent good communication between you and your Duds. Somehow the dress-down Friday relaxation of rules oozed into their minds as relaxation of achievement standards. With their cursory methods—just doing the job quickly with scant attention to detail—the result is often a sloppy product.

As a boss you ask: How can I combat this nonchalance?

What You're Thinking

This is the third time in two weeks I've had to send work back to Felix. That easygoing attitude looks to me like he's not interested or concerned about the quality he produces. I think it's his lukewarm enthusiasm that's responsible for the carelessness. Or maybe he's just spending too much of his workday surfing online. At any rate, he's holding everyone else up, and I've got to do something about it.

A Dud's Thoughts

Why is Jim so hung up on every minute detail? I got the Web design in on time. Now he says I have to do it over. Okay, so I left one minor thing out. Big deal. Who, besides Jim, would know the difference?

STRATEGY

Your goal is to get Duds to adhere, on time, to the standards you set.

1. *Concentrate on resolving the problem.* Forget about figuring out the workers' motives. You'll get further with kindness, such as asking

when something will be ready, rather than demanding it be done by a stated time.

2. *Clarify your instructions.* Review returned work point by point in a nonjudgmental way. Reassure fearful Duds that it's important to ask for help as soon as it's needed, and inform careless Duds precisely what you expect.

3. *Discuss the consequences.* Ask what they think happens when a project is delayed and why they believe they're always late. Explain what can result from the problem. Duds have to understand why and how this difficult situation affects both the company and them personally. They also need to know that your intention is to help them improve.

4. *Work out new procedures together.* Encourage Duds to feel free to suggest or contest. You can reject an idea without rejecting their participation.

5. *Be consistent.* Deliver both praise for good performance and promised consequences for poor work.

TACTICAL TALK

You: *Felix, I'm disturbed that even though you promised to be more careful, you're again being lax about details. Why is that?*

Felix: *I thought it was a good design.*

You: *Your design has three flaws: 1) . . . , 2) . . . , and 3). . . . What this calls for specifically is . . . Do you see how this could be changed to achieve that?*

Felix: *Well, I guess I could tighten it up here by adding. . . .*

You: *Yes, that's a start. It's important that our designs be exact, down to the tiniest detail. Our company's reputation rests on that. If we let careless oversights slip through, we lose our credibility. So we can't* *afford to keep any employee who doesn't pay strict attention to detail. Am I making myself clear about how your job and the company directly affect each other, and about the consequences if this happens again?*

Felix: *You're saying my job is on the line.*

You: *Right. Okay, here's the situation. I'd like you to give this problem some thought, and let's talk again tomorrow. My office, 11 o'clock. I want to hear your suggestions, and then we'll decide how to proceed.*

> **Tip:** After you coach, reassure, and give additional training, you're left with carrying out the promised consequences for uncalled-for delays. Help these Duds move to jobs that better match their abilities, talent, and temperament.

REBELS

Rebels use delaying tactics to get even with you.

Because they're afraid to tell you why they're angry, spiteful Rebels want to get back at you without taking any risks. The tactic they choose is procrastination, using neglect, carelessness, or deliberate misbehavior to result in late and botched-up projects.

Their actions may have been triggered by the way you said something, or by a company policy or procedure they regard as offensive. Whatever it was, it bruised their egos or made them feel inadequate, and they think the safest way to get even is to cause a slowdown in office operations. Interfering with whatever you want done gives them the satisfaction of gaining a measure of control over you.

What You're Thinking

Parker does a pretty good job of hiding his hostility, but I still sense it. I suspect that it was he who intentionally messed up the quarterly report so that it would have to be redone. Also, Parker gave me some lame excuse when he held off placing those important orders. Whenever I want to talk to him, he's taking an extended lunch or out on sick leave. He must know that his delaying tactics are wrong. He's got a good job, good pay, and good benefits. Why is he being a troublemaker? I have to straighten him out.

A Rebel's Thoughts

I was told during my interview that this job would give me a chance to make a difference. Instead I find they settle for substandard results. My boss doesn't seem to care because she takes care of her favorites. Why do we have to adhere to her stupid deadlines when there are so many other factors to be considered? There's no room here for imaginative and creative thinkers who can see more potential for the organization. We're so entrenched in procedures, we don't even know why we're working. The last time I made a suggestion, I got slapped down. I won't risk any more rejection. I'm not a part of what's going on. Well, they can just wait for this stupid report while I take my time and do it over the right way.

STRATEGY

Your goal is to regain control by getting the Rebels to stop hiding their hostility. Until you can get them to speak to you honestly about what's troubling them, instead of resorting to procrastination as tactical revenge, you can't get them back to work.

1. *Blame the system.* Shifting the blame away from them lets Rebels save face and gives them an opening to express themselves. Explain the situation as it appeared to you, and why you consider it a problem. Listen to the response without interrupting.

2. *Ask questions.* Put aside threats and attacks. Successful probing requires a light, friendly tone. Clear the air by making it easy for them to be open and candid with you in a private discussion. In effect, give them permission to unleash their hostility toward you.

3. *Express agreement whenever possible.* Without getting defensive, you can state firmly that you won't allow the operation to be jeopardized. Help them understand why they procrastinate. Together, identify potential ways to handle the situation.

TACTICAL TALK

You: *Parker, the quarterly report is quite late. This presents a problem for our department. How do you suggest I explain the delay to the big boss?*

Or: *Why do you think we had this trouble? Parker, please feel free to be frank. Really, it won't bother me, and I won't hold it against you if you criticize something I've done.*

Or: *You make a good point, Parker. But as you know, we have to turn in those reports on time. What would you recommend to correct this situation?*

> **Tip:** Don't assume that workers who don't criticize openly aren't critical. However, if you give Rebels a chance to clear the air and let them have a say in decisions affecting their responsibilities, most of them will be glad to get back to work.

When your subordinates are procrastinating, don't just sit there and smolder until it's time for their annual evaluation. First, determine why they are causing delays. If they're bored, give them a challenge and a voice to suggest solutions. If they're paralyzed by fear of failure, make it easier and more acceptable for them to ask for help immediately. If they're stalling to seek revenge, get them to articulate the hostility they've been hiding. To maintain your control, you may have to enable your subordinates to feel more freedom on the job and explain how they benefit from achieving your goals.

PART EIGHT

Dealing with Rigid or Obstinate People

Rigidity kills creativity. The two are diametrically opposed. Those who demand that you do things their way because it's the only way wipe out any desire you have to be innovative. Rigid people have trouble adjusting to changing circumstances. Their tenacity and persistence, while admirable in pursuing goals, become detrimental as they hold fast to outdated concepts and antiquated rules.

Unfortunately, almost every office has stubborn bosses, colleagues, and subordinates who just won't bend or budge. They're as stiff as the policies and procedures they claim are carved in stone. Some are severely strict despite the tension it produces.

Such obstinacy may be a cover-up, a way to mask fear, anger, or embarrassment. Most likely, rigid people have backed themselves into a corner and can't get out without losing face. To reach them, you first need to win their trust.

CHAPTER 22

WHEN YOUR BOSS IS UNBENDING

- **Comma Counters**
- **Inflexibles**
- **Pigheads**

At times, bosses are like racehorses wearing blinders to hide their peripheral vision. At other times, they're just plain stubborn as mules.

Some bosses are so rigid about enforcing the fine print, they can't see the handwriting on the wall. Others are obstinate about making modifications even when current conditions cause hardships. Some won't change their minds because pride doesn't permit them to admit that their position spells t-r-o-u-b-l-e.

In any event, you'll never reach the winner's circle by telling bosses they're wrong. They'll only become defensive and even more intractable, especially if you embarrass them in front of others with the facts that prove your case. Even if they agree, they'll get back at you, consciously or subconsciously, at a later time.

Instead, start cultivating a polite, sincere, and relaxed manner. Bosses are more apt to listen when you try to show them how to get what they want while you get what you want.

COMMA COUNTERS

Comma Counters are stubbornly pedantic, demanding perfection in the insignificant.

These bosses have a petty outlook. They see the microscopic parts without also backing up to get a telescopic look at the larger picture. With overemphasis on minor details, they expect precision and undeviating conformity.

The problem for you is that they won't risk trying for a better way. Frequently, they not only lack imagination but also have no *practical* understanding of what's involved in getting your job done.

What You're Thinking

My boss has tunnel vision. He's uncompromising when it comes to adhering to our procedures, clinging rigidly to our scheduling practices. Recent reports of data from other organizations show they are getting more mileage out of their facilities by slightly extending the hours and doubling the shifts. He won't listen. He just stresses the importance of keeping records and filling out forms.

A Comma Counter's Thoughts

Asher is rocking the boat, but I am sticking with something I know I can depend on. The scheduling plan we've been following for years works perfectly fine. Why try something new that might fail if we have something foolproof in place already? I'd better not catch him bending my rules or not completing every last one of the forms on time.

STRATEGY

Your goal is to help your boss get a broader view, a more comprehensive understanding of what's involved. Be straightforward. In a confident, calm, yet enthusiastic tone, convey your sincerity.

1. *Learn the history.* Maybe your boss has been burned before on that issue. If so, let him know that *you* know he's had some experience with this. Express empathy for his needs and concern for how your boss, personally, would be affected if the current practice is continued.

2. *Present authoritative evidence whenever possible.* This is especially important if the boss believes you're asking him to put his reputation on the line. Stress the benefits that will be important to him and your organization, showing why the risk is minimal and how the changes also benefit the boss emotionally.

3. *Scale down your request.* Keep the changes and costs to a minimum. Talk about taking smaller steps over shorter periods of time.

TACTICAL TALK

You: *Boss, my concern is that our current setup is no longer a safe way to go. The drain on our resources is causing. . . .*

Or: *Here's a recent study that shows how well this approach worked in several respected organizations.*

Or: *What if we think about a trial run limited to three months? If there's no marked improvement or if new problems erupt, we can always go back. . . .*

> **Tip:** When bosses ignore larger trends while stubbornly enforcing minor details, contrast the danger of being swept aside with the benefit of going with the flow. Reassure those who bury their heads in the sand, afraid to take risks. Talk about trial testing instead of permanent changes.

INFLEXIBLES

Inflexibles are iron-willed bosses who won't listen and who stick tenaciously to their own ideas.

They are in charge and don't you dare forget it. Their way is the only way because they say so. They rigorously and intolerantly impose unreasonable strictness.

Don't complain to these bosses if this causes you any difficulty. They don't want to hear why it would help you if, just this once, they'd make an exception. Their rigidity is unshakable, their resolve seemingly can't be curved, bent, or diverted. Your problems won't influence them to modify their views. They suddenly can't hear what you're saying, no matter how pointed your comment. They're too busy worrying about keeping control.

What You're Thinking

I want the boss to see that I'm smart and I can come up with good ideas. But I'm getting cold feet about making more suggestions. It's so hard to get her even to consider doing something another way or trying something new. She just wants to indoctrinate us with her ways, to follow exactly in her footsteps. The old ideas are so well insulated, new ideas can't penetrate the stone wall she's built up.

An Inflexible's Thoughts

I've got to watch Savannah a little more closely. I think she's questioning my authority. I can't have any upstart trying to diminish my power by coming up with plans for more participatory management. I'd be a fool to go along with that and lose my control over my workers.

STRATEGY

Your goal is to get your obstinate boss to let a friendly, fresh but critical air flow over your policies and precedents. Your aim is to achieve more open discussions.

1. *Gain insight by pretending.* If I were the boss, what would I want? Understand where the boss is coming from. In presenting your ideas, focus on management's concerns. Explain how your proposal meets the objectives the boss is always talking about. Point up probable consequences if the idea is not accepted.

2. *Explain the mutual benefits.* Explain the benefits not only for the boss and the company but also to you. Let the boss see how eager you are for this plan to work, and what you're willing to give up to make it work (working longer hours, for example). Show your willingness to knock yourself out to make it succeed.

3. *Acknowledge costs and obstacles.* If applicable, prepare a budget and list staffing suggestions. Explain how you'd overcome anticipated roadblocks. Be straightforward, displaying a confidence you may not yet feel.

4. *Go in the back door by creating the market.* Begin by documenting demand, asking opinions from those who'd be using your product or service. When users become caught up with your idea, suggest how they can help you persuade your boss to bring it about.

You: *Boss, I've heard you say how important it is for the company to increase our net. . . . I suppose you've considered consolidating, but how would you feel if we were to combine . . . ?*

Or: *I know it would take quite a bit of time to figure out the logistics, but I'd be happy to do this along with my regular assignment. . . .*

Or: *(To a potential customer.) I'm glad you like the idea. I wonder, would you be willing to help get it off the ground? Would you fill out this brief questionnaire so I could take your thoughts back to my boss?*

Tip: If your boss won't bend, reshape your request and repeat it. People refuse for one reason and agree for another. When bosses are determined to maintain the status quo by practicing thought control, help change their minds by pulling with them instead of against them. Tap into the potential of product or service users by getting them to change the boss's mind for you. Although you've violated no rule, should your boss accuse you of being aggressive, apologize. It's easier to say you're sorry afterward than to get permission from an iron-willed autocrat beforehand.

PIGHEADS

Pigheads hold to a course of action blindly, stupidly, and stubbornly.

They are obstinate, poorly informed, balky bosses who stupidly and persistently adhere to some course of action. They won't listen to your arguments. You can't persuade, plead, or reason with them because to get them to change their course, they'd have to admit they made a mistake.

Pigheads are prejudiced by some preconceived, unreasonable judgment they made before they had the facts and now, although the facts contradict their initial opinion, they won't budge. You feel trapped because your boss's bullheaded directives don't mesh with the tasks you're supposed to perform.

What You're Thinking

The boss doesn't know what he's talking about. He's too stubborn to listen and learn what's going on here. I have so much more experience than he does, even though he's the one with the flashy title. I'm going to be held responsible for his stupid idea that I know is going to fail. If I follow through, I get the blame. If I don't do it, the boss will dump all the lousy assignments on me.

A Pighead's Thoughts

I may not have had actual experience in contacting new clients, but I studied the subject and I resent Ashley's arguing with me over the procedure to use. I've told all my people that I insist on everyone doing this according to my plan. If I let Ashley change the orders I gave her, that would be admitting her way is better than mine. I can't do that. It would be too embarrassing.

STRATEGY

Your goal is to refuse a direct order without causing resentment or being insubordinate. You want restrictions eased so that you can do your job with minimum interference and, hopefully, gain the boss's approval.

1. *Present a substitute to the boss's plan.* Get new ideas from mentors, networks, seminars, or an online search, then ask the boss again. If you don't have time to prepare a full counterplan, you can still

better the odds for success. Slip some sound suggestions into the boss's obnoxious order.

2. *Attempt to solve the boss's problem.* Before you present your idea, ask yourself how it would help cope with cutting costs, increasing sales, or minimizing mistakes. Most bosses follow the "What's in it for me?" principle, so show him, specifically, how your solution helps him.

3. *Add an emotional appeal.* Link your idea to a personal longing. Do you think the boss wants to feel more secure, get more recognition, have more free time, or find a stage to show off some skill?

4. *Act as though you expect acceptance.* Your boss is more apt to agree if you anticipate agreement rather than hostility. Positive expectations encourage positive responses. Attribute to the boss traits he'd like others to think he has.

5. *If the boss won't budge, obey the order precisely.* Don't criticize, but do get the order in writing to protect yourself. Create an electronic paper trail. Document all your actions to show you were following the boss's orders. If you're lucky, your bullheaded boss could eventually get kicked out or transferred. If not, you've continued to do good work, armed against unfair accusations.

TACTICAL TALK

You: *Boss, following your line of thinking, it seems that you're saying . . . (Insert your improvement. It's worth a try.)*

Or: *I know you aren't aware of the situation because if you were, you wouldn't allow this decline to persist. What do you suggest we do, Boss? What would you think about . . . ?*

Or: *Boss, I know you're a reasonable person and the other directors ought to recognize your efforts to make the company more . . .*

Or: *I've summarized our discussion in this email to make sure we proceed the way you want.*

Or: *(You slipped in some changes and the boss balks.) Okay, I'll send a recap email correcting the items you pointed out. I'll wait for your reply before starting the work to make sure we're on the same page. (Once he replies, the boss, not you, will be held responsible.)*

Tip: Do all you can to let your boss save face. Bolster him instead of saying he's wrong. Ask if doing something else might help. When a pigheaded boss refuses to budge and your experience and instincts tell you that you're in jeopardy, survival requires that you protect yourself. Written records and signed instructions become a bulletproof vest. An email paper trail has the added advantage of a time stamp. Plus, you can always forward that email thread to the head executive, if needed.

Concentrate on the wants of rigid and obstinate bosses. If you hit the right button, they themselves will find justification for doing what you suggest. If bosses believe that you are really sincere in wanting to help them, that you've somehow tied your future with theirs, then they'll begin to trust you. The stubborn walls will start tumbling down.

CHAPTER 23

WHEN YOUR COLLEAGUES ARE UNBENDING

- **Killjoys**
- **Chapter and Versers**
- **Stiff-Necks**

Rigid teammates bury their emotions. That allows them to treat other people as things to be placed or pigeonholed. That lets them appear uncaring about your strengths and weaknesses and inconsiderate of your feelings. Their tunnel vision is centered only on the concept or issue or regulation they want you to accept or follow.

To get stubborn colleagues to see another track beside the one they're on, stop looking for "either your way or my way" solutions. Hopefully, through collaboration, you can resolve the matter to your *mutual* satisfaction. Rather than one winning and the other losing, practice negotiating so that both of you get what you're after.

KILLJOYS

Killjoys give you moral or official reasons why it's wrong to enjoy the work.

Killjoys are doggedly determined to sap the pleasure out of anything you're working on. Their remarks take away every last drop of fun you used to get from working in the office.

Because Killjoys are angry, resentful, or bitter, they make it impossible to lighten up. They stringently limit their subordinates and try to carry over their rigidity to you, their peers. They won't let anyone enjoy a relaxed and pleasant working environment.

What You're Thinking

Telling Nick to stop being so restrictive is like telling him to stop breathing. For some reason he's feeling terribly unhappy, and he's taking it out on everybody around him. Is that how he copes with unhappiness? Okay, so he's got some problem that's overwhelmingly complicated. Does that mean he can't allow other people to enjoy themselves while he's miserable?

A Killjoy's Thoughts

We're being paid to produce, not to have fun. What's the matter with these people? I try to tell them the right thing to do, and they give me the silent treatment or they walk away. It's embarrassing to be left standing there alone. I feel so isolated in this office. Nobody ever includes me when they go out to lunch or asks me to join them for coffee. Well, at least now I've got them paying attention to me.

DEALING WITH RIGID OR OBSTINATE PEOPLE

Your goal is to improve the office climate by reducing the tension and bringing the Killjoys back into the fold.

1. *Be a friend.* Their rigid behavior makes you want to isolate them. Your isolating them makes them more rigid. Break the cycle. Be willing to be the good listener, a sponge that sops up the anger and hurt that spills out.
2. *Help them find answers.* Ask questions that get them to identify their viable alternatives for resolving their difficulty. Help the Killjoys get back on course.
3. *Use laughter and gentle teasing.* Laugh, not in derision but in amusement, at their solemnity and rigidity. Play back their words. It's easier for them to say you misunderstood them than to admit they're wrong.

TACTICAL TALK

You: *Nick, you seem upset. Is there anything I can do to help you?*

Or: *Well, how do you think that could be counteracted? Nick, what would it take?*

Or: *It's possible I didn't hear you right, but, Nick, do you know what you just said? You said that . . . Did you mean to come across that way?*

> **Tip:** You don't have to suffer with the Killjoys. If you didn't have a choice, you'd be stuck with accepting their dogmatism. But you do have alternatives that can lessen the tension. To expand your options, look at your need to reduce the stress and restore a pleasant climate. While it's a normal reaction to get back at Killjoys, it has the opposite effect and increases the strain. Try another tactic—*help* the Killjoys to remove their dark clouds.

CHAPTER AND VERSERS

Chapter and Versers know—and quote—every company rule and regulation.

Each policy and procedure is committed to memory. Touch on any topic and these colleagues will spout another executive order. Their knowledge is so detailed, itemized, and precise that they can recite the exact wording of every directive or taboo ever committed to the papers they shuffle.

Chapter and Versers are rigidly unfeeling. They seem to be numb to any personal needs and firmly unyielding when it comes to obeying the letter of the law.

What You're Thinking

We don't need a manual when Erica is around. She's a self-proclaimed guardian of our procedures. Who appointed her the office cop? Every time the discussion deviates from our directives, she's ready to pull us back. Maybe we'd come up with good recommendations, but her one-track mind discourages us from even trying.

A Chapter and Verser's Thoughts

There's a right way and a wrong way to go about this. I can't understand why they don't follow the rules that have been set forth. Why are they being so stubborn? Yes, here it is, the order I told them about. Maybe if I show it to them in writing, they'll see. . . .

STRATEGY

Your goal is to work in a more relaxed manner by getting the Chapter and Versers to loosen their grip on all those rules.

1. *Get them to go beyond what is to what might be.* Only when you do this will their droning stop and your mutual resentment dissipate.

2. *Appeal to Chapter and Versers' self-image.* Talk about the way they see themselves, as the organized, efficient group's memory.

TACTICAL TALK

You: *Erica, you have so much knowledge that could benefit us, and I'm sure you want to. Now, after we all explore the possibility of realigning, why don't you help us organize the results of our brainstorming? Your efficiency can turn all those loose ideas into neatly compartmented platters we can serve the boss.*

 Tip: Don't let Chapter and Versers lace your creative efforts into a straitjacket. Win them over by promising to enlist their computer brains *after* you look for better ways.

STIFF-NECKS

Stiff-Necks are inflexible, arrogant coworkers who say they always did it this way and they always will.

These dogmatic colleagues don't need proof to preach that their opinions are correct. They are totally unbending in their beliefs and self-righteous (almost snobbish) in articulating them.

Stiff-Necks refuse to change. They want to preserve the status quo, whatever the cost.

What You're Thinking

Ruby thinks if you don't agree with her, you're wrong. You become the enemy. She doesn't see the subtle changes that are taking place in the market. There are trends and patterns emerging that Ruby refuses to acknowledge. We can't let her horse-and-buggy ideas influence our decisions and hold us back.

A Stiff-Neck's Thoughts

If they knew a little more about the background of the organization, they wouldn't be so quick to want to change our policies. We struggled hard to get where we are. We went through the testing stages from which good, appropriate decisions evolved. I know we're on solid ground now. What they're suggesting is too risky.

STRATEGY

Your goal is to move in the direction that's best for your organization. This will take open-minded discussions and a willingness to examine all the facets and viewpoints.

1. *Stick to the issues.* Raise the level of discussion when it sinks to personal attacks. Sooth the wounded feelings of Stiff-Necks who take the disagreement as an insult to themselves.

2. *Let the Stiff-Necks salvage their pride.* Let them save face so that they *can* change their minds. Give them a gracious way out.

TACTICAL TALK

You: *Ruby, from what you've told us about your experiences, I can see why you feel as you do. Please explain to us the importance of maintaining. . . .*

Or: *We understand you regard Oscar's proposal as too progressive. Specifically, how would you compare your position to Oscar's?*

Or: *It seems to me that the two positions aren't really that far apart. We all agree that 1) . . . , 2) . . . , and 3) . . . , and we disagree on 1) . . . and*

2) . . . Let's examine those last two points again. Maybe by putting our heads together, we can come up with a better possibility.

Tip: Sometimes it's necessary to gently massage the Stiff-Necks to get them to act cooperatively. They cling to the status quo because it makes them feel secure. Let them feel that you respect their opinions and that they have a part in moving the group from the old position.

When rigid, obstinate colleagues bring about tense situations, it's tempting to walk out or move to another part of the room, or better yet, to tell them off and embarrass them. But such responses only make matters worse. For your own sake, to help make your office a more comfortable place to be, disagree in a pleasant and friendly fashion. Bring them in instead of shutting them out.

CHAPTER 24

WHEN YOUR SUBORDINATES ARE UNBENDING

- **Silent Screwups**
- **Stubborn Mules**
- **Clingers**

Rigid and obstinate subordinates, like Mary, Mary, are quite contrary. They are growing a garden of goofs because they persist in some error or stubbornly stick to some procedure even though you've shown them a better way. If they oppose a rule, they ignore your orders for as long as they can get away with it.

These subordinates aren't anxious to hear any advice you have to give them. If you can't leave them alone, they want you to feel sorry for them or compliment them, anything but tell them how to do their jobs. Their dogged and often unreasonable resistance makes them hard to handle.

SILENT SCREWUPS

Silent Screwups need help but are too proud or stubborn to ask.

They have false pride. They are usually ashamed to ask for help.

They're afraid that their receiving assistance will somehow jeopardize their job.

As a result, they chronically botch up their assignments. They persist in doing something that may be wrong because they won't ask first for more information or some support. They can't understand that it's smart to get help, and their poor judgment in stubbornly insisting that they go it alone results in unnecessarily inept performance.

What You're Thinking

It's so hard to get through to Chase. He acts as if everyone were expected to know everything about every phase of our operation. By the time I finally realized that he was having trouble with his assignment, we lost a lot of valuable time. Why was he so stubborn about coming to me earlier?

A Silent Screwup's Thoughts

The boss is nice to me and I hate to disappoint him. But sometimes I can't figure out what he expects me to do, especially on jobs I haven't handled before. Sometimes I fake it and it turns out okay; other times, it's a mess. But if I ask the boss for more explanation or somebody to help me, he'll know I'm not as good as he thought I was. He'll send me back to my old department.

STRATEGY

Your goal is to bolster the self-concept of Silent Screwups so that they feel secure enough to ask for help just as soon as they need it. Afraid or ashamed, they won't open up until they feel less vulnerable.

1. *Be clear about your expectations.* Demonstrate your patience and reasonableness in anticipating their growth, along with being ready, willing, and able to help. Assign tasks that can develop their weak skills or increase their learning experience. Role-play situations they

find difficult to handle. Suggest online tutorials and other self-improvement resources. Increase the frequency of your feedback.

2. *Be sure your instructions are crystal clear.* Supplement your verbal orders with written instructions. Include deadlines for every step, exceptions to the rules, who or where to turn to for help, what equipment or data to use, and how to report the progress. Have them send you a recap email to ensure understanding and to promote accountability.

3. *Help the Silent Screwups accept responsibility.* Encourage their coming in early for help, but when they do, stretch their minds. Instead of telling them what do, ask for their ideas on how to solve the problem.

TACTICAL TALK

You: *Chase, I really believe you have the potential to go as far as you want in this organization. I want to help you because I think you're worth the time and effort. However, if I'm going to succeed in that, we're both going to have to make some changes.*

Or: *I sent you a zip file with all the information you need for your next assignment. Let's review each document and discuss how you think you should proceed.*

Or: *What do you think you might need to finish it? Have you thought about doing . . . ? Do you think it would help if . . . ?*

> **Tip:** Silent Screwups need your reassurance that it's a sign of wisdom to know what you don't know, admit it, and get help. They aren't goof-offs and they don't want to mess up. They just stubbornly refuse to open up until you assist them in overcoming their fear or embarrassment.

STUBBORN MULES

Stubborn Mules are rigid sticklers for following agreements—overdoing their preciseness.

They can't or won't try to comprehend exceptions to the rule or mitigating conditions. As circumstances change within an office, they refuse to go with the current flow. Instead, they stubbornly cling to the old way of operating.

Stubborn Mules can be exceptionally fine workers. But if you allow them to dictate office policy, you turn up the tension level and increase complaints as the rest of the staff experiences resentment and frazzled nerves.

What You're Thinking

Diana is definitely the best hygienist in my dental practice, but she's awfully stubborn. Since we became a paperless office, she has refused to enter her patients' appointment information in the system. Another staff person has to stop whatever she's doing to input the data. Diana staunchly insists that going paperless is a waste of everyone's time and energy. What we're asking her to do is faster and more efficient than the paper entries she was used to. It's not complicated, but she won't budge. My other employees resent her attitude, and this is causing a lot of problems in the office.

A Stubborn Mule's Thoughts

The boss hired me as a hygienist. That's what I do and I do it extremely well. I wasn't employed to use computers. I don't even own a laptop or an iPad, and I'm perfectly content doing things the old way. I'm afraid whatever I touch, I'll punch the wrong keys and wipe out important information. Everyone else here is comfortable with new technology.

They're always texting and emailing and surfing the Web. It's too embarrassing for me to talk about being so far behind the times. Besides, I don't think I should be forced to follow a new system that wasn't in our original agreement when I was hired.

STRATEGY

Your goal is to reduce the tension in your office by getting the Stubborn Mule to unbend or at least compromise.

1. *Find a time to talk privately.* The best time is probably after everyone else has left the office.
2. *Ask probing questions.* Be calm, cool, and collected. Learn why the worker is being difficult. Often, being annoyed, angry, or frightened can lead to this obstinate behavior. Get the criticism to surface so that you can deal with troublesome perceptions.
3. *Reexamine your procedure.* Maybe you should have offered training before starting the new routine. Possibly the personal as well as organizational benefits were never explained to the Stubborn Mule.
4. *Gently tease.* Poke a little fun at yourself if you joke about rigidity. Don't tease only the rigid person.

TACTICAL TALK

You: *Diana, I hope you know how much I admire and appreciate the quality of your work.*

Diana: *Thank you for saying that.*

You: *You seem a little tense lately. I'm concerned about you. Is there anything happening in the office that's bothering you?*

Diana: *It's like I told you before. I was hired to be a hygienist, not to work a computer.*

You: *I'll never forget when I got my first laptop. I was convinced that whatever I touched, I would break something. I felt like such an idiot. Do you find the computer intimidating, too?*

Diana: *Yes, I guess I do. Knowing I'm not alone does make me feel better.*

You: *Diana, to control your own career, it's important that you're up on the latest developments in computer skills. In that way, you'll always be in demand or can accept a better job, although I'd hate to lose you. I know you'd rather enter patient information by hand than in the computer. But what if I were to work with you—just the two of us? No one else has to know. You can practice as long as you need to until you feel comfortable. And you won't do it solo until you're ready. Do we have a deal?*

Diana: *Well, I suppose I could give it a try.*

Tip: To move the immovable, dig beneath the hard-rock stance to find the culprit. An unreasonable attitude could stem from nursing an ancient hurt or harboring an exaggerated fear. Expose it to dispose of it.

CLINGERS

Clingers commit themselves to inadequately thought-out ideas and won't let go.

They hold on tenaciously to some opinion or proposal. In their stubborn firmness, they ignore logic. They hold fast because they've become emotionally attached to an idea or procedure. Stubborn and intractable, Clingers are particularly difficult to supervise because they go off half-cocked. They hastily and prematurely decide on a course of action without adequate preparation, then feel they have to stay glued to that decision.

What You're Thinking

I wish Gavin would analyze the issues more thoroughly and methodically before jumping to conclusions. He gets overly enthusiastic about an idea without fully comprehending what's involved. Sometimes, with a little bit of luck, it works out okay. On other occasions, by the time he realizes that he moved too quickly, he's in too deep. To get out would be embarrassing, so he stubbornly holds on and tries to make it work. At times he can maneuver all of us enough to help save the day. At other times, the combination of unrealistic optimism and stubborn pride is a disaster.

A Clinger's Thoughts

I know the boss thinks I get too carried away with some of my ideas, but if I sit around and wait for more studies to be done, I'd never get anywhere. If it feels right, you have to move on your instincts and take the risks. If it doesn't work out, I can usually salvage something without having to admit I made a mistake.

STRATEGY

Your goal is to help Clingers balance their optimism by giving their proposals more careful consideration before they act.

1. *Be consistent in what you expect.* If some subordinates tend to oversimplify the problems and get themselves in positions they can't back out of, you may need to be firm. Demand that they first clearly define the problem and ask enough questions to spell out the many facets of the issues. If they learn to look before they leap, there will be less clinging to hastily and poorly conceived ideas.

2. *Discuss consequences in advance.* They can't learn to be responsible if you assume their obligations and bail them out of difficulties. Talk about worst-case scenarios and ask the Clingers what they would do "if . . ." Get them to include in their planning ways to avoid trouble spots or overcome obstacles. This will free them from stubbornly holding on to a bad call out of pride or embarrassment.

3. *Shift the focus.* Move from harping on what they're doing wrong to what is needed to improve themselves. Convey an understanding and trusting tone.

TACTICAL TALK

You: *Gavin, you may have something very good here, but it's important that you get a better handle on the situation. Do a little more research, and be prepared to answer the who, what, when, where, why, and how questions before you go any further.*

Or: *This looks good, but we ought to be prepared for potential snags. What would you do if supplies aren't here on the promised date and the . . . ?*

Or: *Gavin, your ideas are exciting, and I want you to keep coming up with them. Once you put them on a more solid foundation, you'll have real winners.*

> **Tip:** Help Clingers maintain their enthusiasm without jumping the gun. When optimism gets out of hand, ideas need the careful inspection of pessimists for balance and to achieve a realistic plan. Once Clingers have given advanced thought to what could go wrong, they can plan for it or change course without having to cling stubbornly to a losing proposition.

Fear, false pride, annoyance, and anger are largely responsible for subordinates acting rigid and obstinate. You can best cope with these attitudes and improve the climate in your office by helping your workers to feel more secure. Put greater stress on clearly communicating your instructions and expectations, offering genuine support and improved feedback, listening for signs of hostility, and giving them a way out when they feel their pride is tied to their stubborn stance.

PART NINE

Dealing with Tight-Lipped or Uncommunicative People

How exasperating it is to try to get a discussion going when the other person cuts you off with a clipped "yes" or "no" or becomes totally mute. You can't communicate unless both of you listen *and respond* to what you heard or think you heard.

Some uncommunicative bosses, colleagues, and subordinates are simply contemplative types who need time to come to a conclusion. They may be quiet types who keep thoughts to themselves, not commenting if what you're saying doesn't interest them. They easily become responsive, however, when you pose relevant, direct, open-ended questions.

More difficult are the taciturn types who are afraid to open up. Maybe you've hurt their feelings, but they depend on you for their security. Maybe their keeping your good opinion of them looms so large that they can't let a word out. Some are silent and stone-faced for fear that if they reveal their emotions, you'll think they're out of control. Tight-lipped people clam up, sulk, stare, or grin to hide what they're thinking. Getting any of them to express their thoughts is a tough challenge.

CHAPTER 25

WHEN YOUR BOSS IS UNCOMMUNICATIVE

- **Icebergs**
- **Clams**
- **Evaders**

Y ou don't know where you stand if bosses aren't telling you. The word *feedback* is not in their vocabulary. Furthermore, you don't know if they're silent because they're displeased with your work but just don't want a hassle. They could be angry at you and expect you to read their minds.

Maybe the silence has nothing to do with you. Perhaps they're just secretive types who keep their thoughts tightly wrapped because they don't want to have to defend their decisions.

Whether bosses are unsociable, unresponsive, or evasive, their silence makes you feel, at the least, uneasy. Some of you allow their attitude to gnaw at your nerves until you are literally worried sick.

ICEBERGS

Iceberg bosses are unsociable, aloof, and uninterested in exchanging thoughts.

They are so cold you feel the shivers go up and down your spine as they approach. It's true that some bosses deliberately try to intimidate you, using stony silence the way bullies use loud threats. But Icebergs are not out to scare you or subdue you. They're not even thinking about you. They are merely reserved, undemonstrative, secretive people who've decided to button their lips.

You are often dealing with a loner, at least as far as decision making is concerned. Icebergs don't want your input. They don't care to share their plans or justify them to you. They're not interested in your arguments because they've already made up their minds.

What You're Thinking

If you can count the daily "good morning" grunt, the boss hardly says two words to me. I don't think he's angry at me. It's more like I hardly exist. No matter how hard I try, I'm just not very important to him. He's as cold as ice!

An Iceberg's Thoughts

The operations seem to be progressing very well. I hope no one wants to see me this morning, because I have some important decisions to make and I don't want to be disturbed.

STRATEGY

Your goal is to get the boss to open up and to be reassured that you're on the right track.

1. *Find some way to help your boss and thereby help yourself.* You don't have to become best friends; you just want the boss to feel friendly toward you. What do most bosses need? More time, less work, and good news.

2. *Look for time-savers.* In your own little niche, go over every step that involves the boss. Can you make your emails more succinct? Can you quantify and qualify data so that it's easier for the boss to utilize the information?

3. *Look for work-savers.* Is there some task you could offer to take over because it really doesn't require the boss's high-level decision making? Are there items that can be combined for an easier and sharper review by the boss? Remember that some unsociable people prefer texts and emails to in-person dialogue. Try communicating these work-savers this way, and see if the boss is more receptive.

4. *Look for morale boosters—yours and the boss's.* Accept your boss the way he is without taking his aloofness as a personal affront. Keep your finger on the office pulse. If you're not getting the latest news from the boss, get it from the grapevine. Recount to your boss positive reactions you've observed. Study your professional or trade journals to extract and report encouraging signs or trends.

TACTICAL TALK

You: *Boss, I think we could shave quite a bit of time off our staff meetings by distributing background data on agenda items in advance. . . .*

Or: *Boss, if it meets your approval, I'd be happy to draft and email you the executive summary for your review.*

Or: *Gloria, I'm glad you could meet me for lunch. I wanted to ask if you're having any luck getting through to the boss. . . . Could you fill me in on what's happening with . . . ?*

> **Tip:** You have to pay the price to melt the ice. Exert more effort to meet whatever it is the boss needs to develop mutual understanding and respect. When Iceberg bosses play their cards close to their vest and refuse to deal you in on their plans, your move is to earn their trust and make them your friends. Unless you win their confidence, the Icebergs' frigidity will keep you at a distance.

CLAMS

Clams are unresponsive and refuse to tell you why they're silent.

Like the mollusks they are named for, these bosses retreat into their hard shells and clam up. They won't divulge what you want to hear. Their silence is intimidating because you don't know what it means. Your self-confidence erodes. You sweat and fret from lack of feedback.

Unlike Icebergs, Clams may use silence manipulatively. The absence of sound makes you feel uncomfortable and you start to blabber. You rush to stop the hush, spilling out information that you might otherwise not reveal.

Perhaps being uncommunicative is the Clams' means of avoiding commitment. But there's no point in guessing their motives when what you need is data on how you're doing.

What You're Thinking

I worked hard on that plan and I thought it was a darn good idea. Now I'm beginning to lose faith in my own judgment. Perhaps the boss needs more information before reaching a conclusion. On the other hand, maybe the boss doesn't like the idea or resents my coming up with ideas.

Was it a bad suggestion or bad timing? Does his silence say that my work is acceptable or that I'm incompetent? Is he still considering it? I don't have a clue, because the boss isn't talking. How can I crack the shell?

A Clam's Thoughts

Brody's plan has some merit, even though he hasn't had as much experience as I have dealing with that issue. But it's too early to commit myself. I don't want to say anything one way or another until I do some Internet research.

STRATEGY

Your goal is to restore your confidence by getting some good, useful feedback.

1. *Use questions to pry the Clam open.* Avoid queries that can be answered with a yes or no nod. Without pressuring, ask open-ended questions. Go after detailed, specific information.

2. *Don't move a muscle until the Clam responds.* Look directly at the boss, ask your question, then wait, smiling—without uttering another word—until you get a reply. Turn the tables and use the silence to your advantage. Don't rush your Clam, who may be deep in thought, weighing your words before reaching a decision.

3. *Use body language as encouragement.* Nod to show active listening, but let the Clam talk.

4. *Acknowledge the boss's authority—don't threaten it.* Present your ideas as considerations, then ask the boss how to proceed.

TACTICAL TALK

> **You:** *Boss, since you haven't said anything yet about my plan, I assume you need more time to assess it. On which topics would you want*

additional information? Are you concerned about . . . ? How do you feel about . . . ?

Or: *Boss, last week you listed several objectives. I believe I could make better use of my time if I know which ones are tagged as your top priority.*

Tip: Forget about psychoanalyzing bosses who clam up. If you don't get the feedback you need, generate some useful responses. Stop acting intimidated. If you'll carefully think through your questions before you ask, you'll be able to stay calm and composed. The underlying message that you send should be: We're on the same team, so what can I do to help you?

EVADERS

Evaders won't discuss issues because they dislike and avoid confrontation.

These bosses are nice people but can be weak leaders. They don't like arguments and, consequently, won't discuss, debate, or dispute. They keep still because if they don't say what they're thinking, no one can think they're wrong.

Some became Evaders after they overcommitted themselves instead of saying no. In trying to avoid hard feelings or a fight, they ended up breaking their promises and causing the friction they were trying to avert. Evaders refrain from criticizing even when they're angry that something isn't done the way they want. Confronting the issue might make them look as though they were out of control. To them, it's safer to be silent.

What You're Thinking

I asked the boss what she thought about the new method of figuring depreciation. All I got was generalities, nothing specific that I could work with. What should I do when I'm not getting the guidance I need? Should I go over her head? Should I stick my neck out and make my own decision?

An Evader's Thoughts

I didn't give Charles a direct answer when he asked my opinion of the new method. I could see he was spoiling for a fight. Well, he can just take his aggression out on someone else. Besides, it will help develop his character to do more research and think something through for himself.

STRATEGY

Your goal is to force the Evader to come out in the open. If there's hostility, you both have to deal with it and get it resolved.

1. *Make an appointment with your boss.* Don't go into any detail. Just schedule ten minutes of the boss's time. You can't keep avoiding each other or dismissing the fact that you're not communicating.

2. *Get directly to the point of the meeting.* After expressing your desire to attain your mutual objectives, state what you are sensing. Be frank but friendly, and be very careful not to show any signs of annoyance.

3. *Send an email clearly stating what you plan to do.* If you still get no answer, and upon hearing no objection, do it. Move slowly. If you're not stopped, move a little more, but keep your boss informed. (Of course, if your boss objects, you'll stop. But at least you got your Evader to give you some direction.)

TACTICAL TALK

You: *Boss, I know we both want our operation to be as cost-conscious and efficient as possible, so I think we really have to talk about the best ways to achieve our mutual goals.*

Or: *I think I may have inadvertently upset you, and if I have, Boss, I apologize. However, I don't know what I've done wrong or what you may want me to do to correct it.*

> **Tip:** When dealing with Evaders, you have to force their hand, because they'll go to any length to avoid an argument. If you sense hostility, be particularly tactful and composed in order to get the matter discussed. If you feel your boss is afraid of taking risks, supply more concrete or dependable information.

Tight-lipped and uncommunicative bosses are particularly frustrating because they may or may not be reacting to something you did or didn't do. But it's not good for you to continue working under the stress of uncertainty. You must get your boss to open up. The best way is to take the initiative and politely, professionally ask open-ended questions that can give you the direction you're seeking.

CHAPTER 26

WHEN YOUR COLLEAGUES ARE UNCOMMUNICATIVE

- **Skeptics**
- **Withholders**
- **Glarer-Starers**

You work side by side with colleagues who won't talk to you. You try, but you can't get through. Sometimes you get the feeling that they mistrust you, although you believe you've acted honorably. Some coworkers are uncooperatively silent when you can't remember doing anything that might have offended them. Others let you know they are angry—they send you fierce and fiery looks—but they won't disclose why. They won't utter a word.

You've concluded that these colleagues are nursing hurt feelings. Apparently, they're annoyed or angry at something you said or did. However, their messages aren't clear and it's difficult to concentrate on your work amid their negative vibrations.

SKEPTICS

Skeptics are suspicious. They look for some proof before opening up to you.

Skeptics are not hostile or cold, yet they are barely lukewarm. They don't know if they can trust you. That makes them hesitate before they'll commit or confide.

They question your intentions, doubt your sincerity, and wonder if you're hatching some plot. As far as they're concerned, the jury is still out on your case. In the meantime, the climate in your office is getting a little sticky and damp.

What You're Thinking

I wonder why Ian reacts so slowly and begrudgingly when I make a suggestion or comment. I get the feeling that he's questioning my motives. But I'm not sure because he so seldom speaks to me and, when he does, it's usually a one-word response. I think it would help us both if we could talk.

A Skeptic's Thoughts

I'm still not sure about Levi. I don't know what he's up to or if I can depend on him. He suggested I join him in preparing that report. If I do, will I get left holding the bag? I'd better play it safe and remain noncommittal with Levi. The less I say to him, the better, at least for now.

STRATEGY

Your goal is to convince Skeptics that you truly aim to help your group, department, and company. Show that your suggestions are not meant as self-serving.

1. *Supply evidence of your good faith.* Let your good idea become "ours" rather than "mine." Report to Skeptics useful news they may not have heard. When you finish your work early, offer to help them.

2. *Be up-front.* Explain the mutual benefits more carefully, but don't hide the obstacles. Make a promise and keep it. Inspire confidence by your reassuring attitude.

3. *Nudge, don't push.* Be willing to move slowly and gently instead of aggressively. Be sincere and honest in expressing compliments and appreciation.

TACTICAL TALK

You: *Ian, I'm through with my deliverables for the day. Can I give you a hand? Did you hear the latest ruling that just came down from the big boss?*

Or: *I know you can see why it would be time-saving, but I should point out a couple of potential problems. Maybe you can suggest how we can go around the roadblocks.*

Or: *Take your time. There's no rush. But I really would appreciate hearing your opinion.*

> **Tip:** Trust isn't earned overnight. It's a slow, protracted process to persuade Skeptics that you're for real. If you've been pushing too hard, show more patience by first laying a good foundation for the trust you want them to bank on.

WITHHOLDERS

Withholders hold back from telling you the information you need.

Withholding is a form of sulking in disguise. Withholders usually know more than you do about a given subject and are hurt that you haven't acknowledged their expertise. Consequently, in order to make you come to them, they tell you none or only part of what you have to know.

They won't cooperate until you verbalize your recognition and appreciation of their knowledge. Their buttoning up is a frustrating tactic, but it sure gets your attention.

What You're Thinking

Gretchen has finished making the latest projections, but she's not parting with that information. She says it's too soon to be sure she's right, but that's just an excuse not to give us what we need so that we can proceed with our planning. Could it be that she's acting childish and just wants to be begged?

A Withholder's Thoughts

If they want my information, they can show me a little more respect. I'm the most tenured in this office. Plus, I stay late and go over my figures very carefully to be sure they're correct. Then they come by demanding my data without taking the time to recognize my efforts. They are completely uninformed in this area. They need me. You think they'd show some appreciation.

STRATEGY

Your goal is to get Withholders to give you the required information.

1. *Soothe wounded egos.* Couch your request more tactfully. Be more generous with warranted praise and appreciation. Send a group email, sincerely praising the Withholder.

2. *Come in the side door.* When Withholders won't answer your direct request, ask them to confirm your conclusions or the limited facts you were able to gather. Admit your ignorance and ask them to fill you in. Inquire how they would go about tackling your problem.

TACTICAL TALK

You: *Gretchen, I don't know what this team would do without your talent. You're the one who's kept us pointed in the right direction. I'm going to nominate you for employee of the month.*

Or: *I realize you're not ready to share your projections with us, but I wonder if you'd look at this. . . . This is what we think we're facing. Admittedly, we're all not experts on this subject. Maybe you could fill in a few gaps.*

> **Tip:** Give Withholders the credit they deserve. Withholders are sulkers. You've hurt their feelings and they're getting back at you. Remedy the wrong, and the information you need will start pouring right out.

GLARER-STARERS

Glarer-Starers silently express their anger through fixed, hostile looks.

These colleagues bottle up their anger because they're afraid of a fight. Their body language, however, broadcasts their ire or indignation. They act as though you ought to be able to read their minds. That makes no sense, because they give you no clues.

Sometimes Glarer-Starers are so deeply hurt that they are unable to talk about the cause. You try to reach them and you're rebuffed.

What You're Thinking

I asked Julian what was wrong when he started with those contemptuous stares. All day he's been looking right through me as though I'm something less than human. He said nothing was wrong, with a childish pout, as if I'm supposed to know what ticked him off.

A Glarer-Starer's Thoughts

I'm furious at the way Hudson is taking advantage and dumping his extra cases on me. Did I give him any indication that I was looking for more work? I don't think I helped bring about this situation, but I can't confront Hudson about it. I'm so angry, I'm afraid I'll get emotional and start yelling and losing control. That would be unprofessional, and I'll lose everyone's respect.

STRATEGY

Your goal is to get the Glarer-Starers to discuss the problem. If their actions seem childish, then it's up to you to remain in control.

1. *Offer an olive branch.* Show you want to make peace by trying to get the problem out in the open where it can be resolved. Suggest a neutral setting, maybe meeting for lunch.
2. *Be quietly persistent.* If your friendship offer is refused, try again. Keep trying, until eventually the Glarer-Starers reveal what's bothering them. Keep in mind that texts or emails might be better received than in-person requests.
3. *Prepare for the next controversy.* Discuss how you both want to handle disagreements in the future. Take ownership for the roles that you both play in effective communication.

TACTICAL TALK

You: *Look, Julian, wouldn't you agree that up to now we've had a pretty good and honest relationship? I want to preserve that.*

Or: *You say nothing is wrong and that's good. But I feel there is something you want to get off your chest. If something is wrong, I'm sure you'd want us to remedy the problem.*

Or: *In the future, when either of us gets mad, we're going to have to be more frank and straightforward and willing to discuss the situation; don't you agree?*

Tip: While silence and penetrating stares appear to be part of a juvenile approach, sometimes Glarer-Starers are not ready to discuss the problem. They may be deeply hurt, with emotions still too close to the surface. Nevertheless, they usually do want to talk to you, so keep plugging away at being a friend.

Colleagues who figuratively or literally stop talking to you may distrust your motives or feel disappointed, hurt, or angry at something you've done. Since they refuse to tell you what that is, first concentrate on winning back their confidence before you continue playing detective.

CHAPTER 27

WHEN YOUR SUBORDINATES ARE UNCOMMUNICATIVE

- **Grinners**
- **Worrywarts**
- **Tongue-Tieds**

You think you're a good, kind boss, and it surprises you to learn that some of your workers don't feel comfortable with you. They try to hide it, but they're scared. Whatever they ask you, however they respond to your questions, no matter what they do, they are afraid you'll think they're ignorant or foolish or incapable.

The desire to make and maintain a good impression can be so stressful when they think a job is shaky that it inhibits them from talking effectively to you. Fearful of botching their message, they say as little to you as they can get away with. Some won't speak out at meetings because of this fear.

To reach uncommunicative subordinates, it's important to pick up on and respond to their perceptions, wants, and interests before you try to get anything else across to them.

GRINNERS

Grinners won't voice objections; they hide behind a grin when provoked.

They may be hurt or angry but are afraid to speak out because they believe their job depends on pleasing you. They may be hiding their hostility from themselves as well as from you. Little nervous telltale gestures, such as staring at their shoes or out the window, signal that what they are feeling doesn't match the cheerful smile and pleasant words.

Grinners put on a happy face no matter what you ask of them. They are obedient and uncomplaining, and remain passive although they believe they've been pushed too far. You sense something is wrong. You can't quite nail down the incongruity, but you know that eventually you will have to deal with it.

What You're Thinking

I had asked Dorothy to prepare a compilation before Wednesday. On Tuesday morning she turned in a list with one segment missing. I asked her why it wasn't finished. She said nothing and just stood there grinning. So I kept going with, "Well, do you need more time?" "Yes," she replied, and left. I can't figure out what's happening. Dorothy didn't say that she was upset or stymied. Did I say something in anger that may have offended her? If so, why the grin and why isn't she talking to me?

A Grinner's Thoughts

The boss asked me to prepare that compilation knowing full well I would have to get a segment of the information from my old nemesis, Evan. I completed everything except that segment, but I can't tell the boss why. He'd jump down my throat again. I don't feel secure enough to level with the boss. Until I know it's safe to open up, I'll shut my mouth and keep a lid on my real feelings.

STRATEGY

Your goal is to unlock the agony, annoyance, or anger that brought about the silent grin-and-bear-it attitude.

1. *Enable the Grinners to come to you.* When a problem comes up, show you are listening and more concerned with how the work is affected than with verbally thrashing the workers for having the problem. Cool off first if you're angry. Then you can deal with the issue tactfully and directly.

2. *Ask open-ended questions.* Queries that can be answered with a "yes" or "no" stop or discourage discussion. Instead, choose questions that delve into what the Grinners are thinking and feeling, to get a better understanding of their unresponsiveness.

3. *Be still and wait for the reply.* Don't fill the void; don't keep talking to stop the silence. Wait patiently, showing no irritation, until you get a response.

TACTICAL TALK

You: *What do you think caused that, and how can we correct it?*

Or: *How long do you estimate it might take? What other problems might we encounter?*

Or: *What's your opinion about . . . ?*

Or: *How do you feel about . . . ?*

Or: *Do you believe it's an unreasonably short time to complete . . . ?*

> **Tip:** Listen to what isn't said. If the Grinners aren't talking to you, for some reason they feel anxious or threatened. It could be that if they wait long enough to reply—and just stand there grinning—you'll answer your own questions for them.

WORRYWARTS

Worrywarts fool themselves into believing that no feedback from the boss is good news.

They differ from Grinners by not hiding their feelings. Instead they hide behind their computers to avoid conversation.

This assumption, "If I don't ask, you won't tell," could harm their careers. They are not hearing significant criticism that could help them improve performance. And they are missing opportunities to influence the direction of their jobs by not finding ways to talk to you.

Worrywarts begin unconcerned, stoically accepting this lack of communication as a positive sign. Everything must be going great or else you'd be screaming for changes, right? Then they begin to wonder, afraid to hear a critique. The formerly happy worker bounces back and forth between unhappy crab and contented cow.

What You're Thinking

I've been awfully busy lately, but now that the merger is completed, I'd better take the time to review progress with my staff. Fortunately, they need little direction from me. Kent, though, is avoiding me, and seems to be fluctuating, like he's on an emotional elevator. I hate to confront him, but I must find out what's bothering him. I've had too many good workers leave without telling me why.

A Worrywart's Thoughts

It's been a long time since the boss has commented on the work I've turned in. On the one hand, no feedback probably means he's satisfied. My work is good. I don't really need feedback, do I? But where do I stand since the merger? He gave everyone the same brief message. What if I do have a problem? What if I've been doing something wrong?

Am I going to be downsized? I'm afraid to ask him. I'd better leave well enough alone.

STRATEGY

Your goal is to restore the Worrywarts' confidence and to refocus their energy.

1. *Recognize the impact of feedback.* Constant, consistent, constructive feedback is the most important thing your workers need. To withhold it is cruel and uncalled-for punishment, fostering anxiety and fear of asking what's in store for them. Letting terse emails and texts substitute for a give-and-take conversation leaves employees longing and frustrated. Remember that tone and inflection can be easily misinterpreted through a text message or email.

2. *Expand the direction of feedback.* Add to your downward, one-way information an upward flow to achieve true, two-way communication. To reduce anxiety, anger, or resentment, draw out employee thinking and feelings with open-ended questions. Explain changes that are about to be made.

3. *Focus on what you and your workers have in common.* Talk about getting the job done. Let them express what they believe they should be contributing and be held accountable for. This probably differs from your perception, but it provides a basis for working out your differences. A little flexibility on your part can help bring about their acceptance when your way overrules.

TACTICAL TALK

You: *Kent, with the merger completed, there will be some changes. I want to discuss with you how your role may be affected. As you know, one objective is . . . How do you think you might help us achieve that?*

Kent: *(Silence.)*

You: *What specifically do you believe you should be held accountable for? (Then give silence a chance to work. Maybe Kent's thinking about an answer.) . . . Did I catch you off guard?*

Kent: *Yes, you did.*

You: *Are you concerned about how I'll react? What do you think I'll say?*

Kent: *I'm afraid you'll think I'm in over my head. But I'd rather hear criticism than not know how I'm doing.*

You: *Well, let's discuss this some more to decide whether you need additional training.*

Tip: Everyone needs feedback. It's your chance to encourage innovation and unleash talent. Even those who never give you a hard time need it. All workers have to know that they're valued. Without feedback, some good workers can become emotional wrecks and some just go elsewhere. Feedback is especially useful when your approach is to gently draw out the uncommunicative worker.

TONGUE-TIEDS

Tongue-Tieds are inarticulate or shy. They can't seem to verbalize their thoughts.

They are so overly concerned that you think well of them that they are too embarrassed to speak. While their ideas may be worth considering, they're afraid they will sound foolish. You ask for suggestions and they're too timid to answer the impersonal queries.

Some are afraid they might sound boring or dull or unclear. They may think their opinions are neither necessary nor wanted. They suffer stoically rather than verifying their perceptions.

Other Tongue-Tieds are afraid they'll be judged as weak if they ask for help. They won't ask a question that might make them appear ignorant, especially if they believe everybody else understands what's going on.

What You're Thinking

I know Luke is capable of intelligent, even spirited conversation. I've overheard him talking to his own workers. But he gets tongue-tied around me. And he's terribly ill at ease when he has to give a prepared talk, even a short report. That's a shame. If he could get over his reluctance to speak up and speak out, Luke has the potential to go far in this organization.

A Tongue-Tied's Thoughts

I'd like to comment when the boss asks us for ideas, but I'm so scared I'll make a fool of myself. Maybe the others will contradict me; maybe they'll show me up to be wrong. Maybe I won't choose the precise words and I'll seem ridiculous. I'd look like a moron if I asked a question and everybody but me knew the answer.

STRATEGY

Your goal is to help the Tongue-Tieds feel comfortable about talking to you and talking before their peers and other groups.

1. *Encourage their questions.* In private talks, you can help relieve their shyness by reassuring them that we all make mistakes because we're human and need more information. Suggest that for now it

might be easier to participate at staff meetings if they were to write out their questions, and when they get used to that, to add a brief comment before the question.

2. *Ask them direct questions.* At your meetings, turn to the Tongue-Tieds when you reach areas where you know they have experience or expertise.

3. *Help them improve their meeting reports.* Suggest that they practice at home and make a video of themselves. Watching the video can help them to improve their approach and technique.

4. *Assign them to small committees.* The give-and-take discussions in smaller groups are so informal that they serve as good practice sessions. Here the Tongue-Tieds can gain confidence in expressing themselves.

5. *Suggest public speaking courses.* Perhaps your company has a training program in which the Tongue-Tieds can get assistance. If not, point out available community resources, like Toastmasters.

TACTICAL TALK

You: *Luke, I know you're good at putting your finger on the real problem. At the staff meetings, when you ask a question that pinpoints the real issue, you play a most important role in problem solving.*

Or: *(At a meeting.) Luke, you worked on that last year. What do you think about the idea of repeating it again?*

Or: *When you know you have to give a report, don't try to wing it or read it. Write out and memorize only brief opening and closing statements. Then practice at home from a key-points outline. When you know your subject as well as you do, you can do most of your report by answering questions from the group. That almost eliminates your giving a speech.*

> **Tip:** Some Tongue-Tieds need more than reassurance, especially if they're having difficulty with a prepared talk. Explain how this personal problem can hold them back, and offer to help. If you can't coach them yourself, suggest places where they can get assistance.

Uncommunicative subordinates are usually afraid to speak. They are too angry, worried, or embarrassed to try. So it's up to you to encourage them to talk to you without dreading the outcome. Ask questions that will unearth the causes of their concern, and then you can respond to what they're saying. You may need to relax your rigidity, provide better feedback, offer more reassurance, or, in some cases, coach the poor public speaker.

PART TEN

Dealing with Complaining or Critical People

We expect others to be thick-skinned while our own egos are as fragile as egg-shells. If I give you my unsolicited opinion, it's to help you improve. If you give me your unasked-for advice, you're criticizing me. Giving and receiving top-notch criticism is an exceedingly delicate art.

Basically, your critic is saying, "You and I ought to have the same values, but you're not acting according to my standards." That's okay, as long as you respect the other's right to an opinion and stick to dissecting the issues. Difficult bosses, colleagues, and subordinates have never heard of those rules.

With them, you're automatically wrong. They make mincemeat of your dignity. They even singe themselves when making things hot for you. Some skillfully manipulate you with self-incrimination. Others are confirmed complainers who have no intention of fixing what's wrong. They shed their responsibility by telling you about it; now it's your problem.

Nevertheless, since the critics' behavior is predictable, you can plan ahead how to deal with them. You can also learn to be choosy; not every issue is worth doing battle over.

CHAPTER 28

WHEN YOUR BOSS IS A FAULTFINDER

- **Nitpickers**
- **Checklist to Improve Your Listening Skills and Responses**
- **Guilt Ladlers**
- **Hanging Judges**
- **Meat Grinders**

Some bosses are quick to make you their scapegoats. Others rip you apart when you *are* to blame. Only when it's your blunder does it really matter who's at fault. Then you have to own up to your mistake immediately, apologize, and suggest remedial action.

Pointing your finger at another culprit (boss, coworker, or subordinate) only makes you look weak. Sometimes you're not really comprehending what your boss, clients, or customers really want. Whether or not it's deserved, criticism usually stings, and bosses become especially upset when you can prove they were at fault. That forces them to defend themselves and repair their egos. So forget that legitimate excuse. When faultfinding supervisors are manipulative, tyrannical, petty, or wimpy, you can use other tactics to deal with their complaints without coming unglued.

NITPICKERS

Nitpickers always find minor errors. These bosses enjoy bickering about inconsequential details.

You're living up to what you promised to do. Now, in the middle of everything, you're hearing that you have to do an important task over again. If this were a vital element, of course you should. But you believe your boss actually gets a boost out of making molehills into mountains.

What's he afraid of? Why can't he trust you? More important, how do you get the boss off your back?

What You're Thinking

Why is Stan always on my case? Why can't he just leave me alone until I finish, instead of squabbling over petty minutiae? He feels compelled to oversee every detail. He hired me to do a job because I'm capable. Now he picks apart everything I do! How can I convince him to let me complete what I'm doing before he rips my work apart?

A Nitpicker's Thoughts

Looking at the latest reports, I'm convinced more than ever that we have to cut costs. Any mistakes and I'm the one who gets the blame. I can't afford the slightest error. I know I've got a talented team, but I've got to be even more diligent in checking the work they're doing.

STRATEGY

Your goal, being allowed to work more independently, requires reassuring your boss that he can trust you.

1. *Avoid direct criticism of your boss.* A Nitpicker who's obsessed with controlling every detail might react by firing you.
2. *Capitalize on the boss's objections.* Instead of feeling (or worse, displaying) your anger or annoyance, be ready with a positive, reassuring response. Thank the boss for bringing the matter to your attention.
3. *Review your listening skills.* Pick up on what you have missed. Make sure you understood correctly. Be extra careful and double-check your work. Send an email after your in-person dialogue to show your boss that you are on the same page.

TACTICAL TALK

Boss: *This just won't do. We have to change the justification and . . .*

You: *Yes, I understand that you want more emphasis on cost-cutting. And I appreciate your help in resolving this. I know that working together, we'll find the right approach. We could start by . . . and then go to . . . How do you feel about that?*

Boss: *Yes, that's what I was trying to tell you.*

You: *Good. I should be able to make those changes by Thursday. I'll report back to you then. Okay?*

CHECKLIST TO IMPROVE YOUR LISTENING SKILLS AND RESPONSES

Too often, you don't listen because you're so anxious to put in your two cents' worth. You're thinking about your response instead of hearing what's said. You want to get it out before the other person can come up with an argument against it. You miss signals because you're not concentrating. Or you hear only what you expect to hear, because preconceptions and emotional blocks (yours and the speaker's) can distract you.

❏ Do you listen to understand, rather than to prepare a response? If you think you're under attack, listen for the reason behind the attack. You don't have to agree. You can acknowledge without arguing: "Of course you feel you should get what you want, however . . ." Or, if yours was an unintentional slur, this can easily be corrected.

❏ Do you listen without interrupting? If you break in, you're not hearing the entire message. Listen to learn what's important to others. What exactly do they want to know? Then that's what you'll emphasize when it's your turn to talk. Your aim is to link their goal with yours.

❏ Do you listen for main ideas instead of trying to remember all the facts? Do you question any assumptions that are misrepresented as facts?

❏ Can you maintain eye contact and resist looking away from the speaker? Do you give a nod or a smile to show you're interested and paying attention?

❏ Do you watch the speaker's body language? Do face and gestures match the words?

❏ Is there a hidden meaning between the lines?

❏ Do you ask probing questions to get pertinent information? Do you try to draw out thinking, instead of supplying answers, to obtain another's point of view?

❏ Do you ask clarifying questions? Try such nonthreatening queries as: "I don't quite understand. How would that alter . . . ?" or "Would I be correct if I said that your position is one of . . . ?"

❑ Do you restate to be sure you understood? To be absolutely certain, try: "This is what I think I heard you say. . . ."

❑ Do you let others speak first so you can respond initially with a point of agreement? Then you can raise concerns or explain without making excuses.

❑ Do you listen to reexamine your position? Maybe there could be a better way, and you'll want to improve your stand. Or, maybe some ideas could be combined. Listen for a common thread that could link both points of view or help you arrive at a consensus.

❑ Do you patiently let an emotional person unwind before you jump in? People who are angry or upset don't absorb what you're saying. Why kick someone who's already down?

❑ Can you listen respectfully and nonjudgmentally? If you want others to open up, they have to feel that you honestly want to learn what they're thinking and won't pounce on them for what they tell you.

❑ Do you listen supportively so that you can offer good criticism? Concentrate on how you can help promote your boss's agenda—not to enhance the ego, but to get the desired results.

❑ Do you listen to yourself? It's called a third ear, considering how you probably sound to others. Are you aware of your tone and tempo?

> **Tip:** Nitpicking bosses have to trust you before they'll leave you alone to do your work. By becoming a better listener, you can make the insecure feel they have an ally.

GUILT LADLERS

Guilt Ladlers manage to make *you* feel guilty, no matter the real reason.

Guilt Ladler bosses choose a roundabout route to criticize and complain. They use being hurt as a manipulative club over your head. They try to control you by making you feel guilty—you're to blame for their bruised feelings.

As a result, you reproach yourself if you don't do what was asked of you, while getting angry at the boss for asking. But being angry makes you feel more guilty, so you comply. You've just been snared by the guilt trap.

Having convinced themselves that they're blameless, Guilt Ladlers deny responsibility. They've already shunted the problem to you. Although denial increases their guilt, they're unable to apologize. To get relief, they blame others and broadly hint that they deserve to suffer. Wallowing in self-pity, they refuse your help as they lash out at you for not helping.

What You're Thinking

The boss tells me, "Look at what you've done to us. I really expected you to show more diligence. Everyone in our department has always scored highest in that program. What do you think the other managers are going to say now about me and my department? Don't be surprised if I go into cardiac arrest." I feel so drained from having another one of those conversations with the boss. I don't know how he can twist everything around, but he manages to make all of us lose sight of the real issues.

A Guilt Ladler's Thoughts

Gene told me it would be tough for him to carry his regular load and participate in the program, too, but he agreed to do it. He promised me he'd work hard. He ought to know how much it means to me to have the respect and admiration of all the managers. Why did he do this to me? I guess it's my fault for being so trusting.

STRATEGY

Your goal is to get out of the trap that the master manipulator has set for you.

1. *State your feelings clearly.* Be honest about being hurt or disturbed by what the boss has said. You're not criticizing the boss if you simply state how *you* feel, along with your desire to restore the damaged relationship.
2. *Toss back the guilt.* Politely and calmly refuse to accept it. Point out in a straightforward manner the role that the boss has played.
3. *Sever the boss's problem from yours.* The boss is showing signs of insecurity, so be careful to protect the boss's feelings as you do this.

TACTICAL TALK

You: *Boss, I was upset when you said I hadn't been diligent about the program. I've always considered you a fair person, and I believe we've had a pretty good relationship up to now, so I'd like to clear the air.*

Or: *Perhaps you've forgotten our talk, in which we agreed 1) . . . , 2) . . . , and 3). . . .*

Or: *Now, if you want greater participation from our department on that program, may I suggest that we adjust . . .*

> **Tip:** Don't wilt from the guilt. Guilt Ladlers try to shift the blame for their poor judgment or insecurity onto you. They criticize your actions as the cause of their hurt feelings so that you, in turn, feel guilty and they have more control. Refuse to buy the boss's ludicrous look at the world. Politely state the real facts and get on with resolving the problem.

HANGING JUDGES

Hanging Judges blame you before gathering or hearing the facts.

Take your pick of whodunits. The culprit is your boss, your co-worker, or maybe it was a natural disaster. In any event, you are not guilty. But you haven't yet pleaded your case and you're being convicted.

Blaming others for troubles they themselves may have created, Hanging Judges look for scapegoats. If they're at fault for a failing project, they can't admit it. Instead, they seek easily intimidated, vulnerable victims. You are picked because you're not likely to retaliate.

Hanging Judges aren't interested in finding answers. Of utmost importance to them is that they maintain control. To do this, they feel they must rid themselves of the failure tag. So, "Tag, you're it."

What You're Thinking

Wow, is the boss mad! All those accusations and the name-calling! If he's trying to intimidate me, he's doing a great job. But it was he who really caused the catastrophe. If I show him up, he'll resent it. If I don't, I get blamed unjustly. I'm really stuck.

A Hanging Judge's Thoughts

I told Judy to market the new opening to internal candidates before posting the ad online. I also told her to hold off a week before adding any new people. But now what am I going to do? Somebody must have complained to the big boss about this new hire. I'll send Judy a reprimand, telling her to straighten out the mess immediately, with a copy to the big boss. That will let him know I'm right on top of the situation.

STRATEGY

Your goal is to stop being made the boss's scapegoat. You have to stand up for yourself while showing the boss you're more useful as an ally than as a victim.

1. *Let go of your hurt feelings.* Keep still until your anger subsides. To get a little objectivity, back away, pretending it's someone else's problem. In all probability, you're not the only one the boss treats this way.

2. *Deal with the boss's hostility.* Politely show that you're not the weak and vulnerable victim the boss thought you were. To voice your objections, use questions rather than accusations.

3. *Criticize without doubting authority.* If the boss thinks you're questioning his actions, he'll become defensive and immovable. Don't blame *anyone.* Keep your disagreement on a professionally high plane to avoid a confrontation. Be cooperative and respectful, and stick to the issues.

4. *Provide a gracious way out.* After the boss calms down and is rational, discuss objectives and suggest options. Find some points on which you can sincerely compliment and agree with the boss. Help him increase his own self-esteem.

You: *Boss, I don't blame you for being upset. What order did you want me to follow? (Rather than, "It was your order I followed to the letter.")*

Or: *It seems to me that we all got our signals crossed on this one. Maybe we could avoid this in the future if we were to . . .*

> **Tip:** When you're being blamed for something that's not your fault, don't yell "Foul." Keep playing, even though the boss is changing the rules in the middle of the game. But come back strong, in a polite and straightforward manner. It's unlikely you'll get picked on again once the boss realizes you're more valuable as a supporter than as a scapegoat.

MEAT GRINDERS

Meat Grinders are overly candid. Their cutting criticism rips you to shreds.

This time it *was* your fault. There's no way to hide this blunder that may blow your career chances. Panic takes over. Meanwhile the boss, always stern, is furious and unrelenting with her sharp accusations. But this time she has every right to be angry.

Don't answer the charges. Freeze in your tracks. Say, "I'll be right back," and leave the room or hang up the phone. If the criticism is by text or email, put down your smartphone or walk away from your computer. Now take a few deep breaths and remember that everybody makes mistakes. It's how you face up to a mistake that influences your future. Also, keep in mind that bosses have the right to criticize your work, but that doesn't include the right to inflict cruel knockout blows to your ego.

What You're Thinking

I know the boss told me to take care of the Lasser order before I did more work on anything else. I thought it could wait because I had so many other things I had to do that I considered more important. I was wrong. Lasser called, screaming at the boss, and the boss pelted me with her reprimands. She's not just mad; I think she's completely lost confidence in me. This is a mess I brought on myself. If this doesn't cost me my job, I'll be paying for it for years to come.

A Meat Grinder's Thoughts

Wesley really blew it this time. If he lost us that Lasser account, it's going to be the last account he loses. He thinks he's so smart, that he knows more than I do. I just can't depend on him. I don't want to hear his excuses. What a day this has been! First the fight at home, then that idiot in the parking lot, and now this. Why couldn't Wesley follow my orders? Now that it's too late, it might dawn on him that I was right.

STRATEGY

Your goal is to immediately remedy your mistake and get back in the boss's good graces.

1. *Admit your error quickly and emphatically.* As soon as you realize that you, or someone under you, goofed, claim the blame. In the boss's mind, this computes as, "Aha, he sees I was right to criticize him, so I suppose he's not so dumb after all. Let's see what else he has to

say." Denying your mistake only makes you appear spineless. Delaying causes you unnecessary hardship.

2. *Give no alibi or excuse.* If your subordinate was the one who messed up, you still have to accept the responsibility. Get to the point without cushioning the misdeed. You were wrong. You are sorry. An alibi would only make the boss madder because it implies the boss accused you unjustly.

3. *Offer a way to make it better.* Suggest your plan to correct the error. Restate your boss's criticism, transforming each negative into a positive objective. If, after having time to calm down, the boss continues hurling insults at you, hold on to your dignity by proclaiming that you accept the criticism as sound, but that her being unnecessarily rough is delaying progress in working things out.

4. *Seek agreement on the plan.* Whatever you two come up with, be sure you're in accord before you leave. If the boss has to bring in someone else to clean up your dirty work, this won't improve your relationship.

TACTICAL TALK

Boss: *(Yelling.) You never follow orders!*

You: *Boss, I used very poor judgment in not taking care of the Lasser order as you had directed me to do. It was a stupid mistake. I was wrong and I'm sorry.*

Or: *Boss, from now on your orders will be processed 1) . . . , 2) . . . , and 3) . . .*

Or: *I think we can still hold on to Lasser if we tell him that we oversold our new product and . . . Okay, then we agree. I'll go out there this afternoon and straighten it out.*

> **Tip:** Stop predicting doomsday because you made a mistake. Everybody makes mistakes. The real danger is in compounding the error by not saying you're sorry or not apologizing soon enough.

It's a no-win situation to place blame on someone else. In a confrontation with the boss, if you win now, you lose later. Don't blame anyone, unless you're apologizing for yourself. Either way, move quickly to remedy the situation.

Prevention is the best defense against bosses' criticisms—valid or otherwise. Keep them informed, because bosses don't like surprises. Try to involve them in your assignment, especially at the planning stage. Avoid hurting their feelings. They instinctively strike back if you seem to be questioning their authority. Keep your antenna out to pick up on ways to assist them in achieving their personal goals. Bosses you help are less apt to criticize you.

CHAPTER 29

WHEN YOUR COLLEAGUES ARE FAULTFINDERS

- **Squawkers**
- **Supersensitives**
- **Checklist for Dealing with Supersensitives**
- **Wisecrackers**
- **Wet Blankets**

Critical colleagues are treasured gems when they help you develop better insight and discover new possibilities. But many of your peers don't listen supportively or bother to cushion their comments. They may have nothing against you personally, but they complain in general. Others react resentfully if they think you're criticizing them.

Usually, faultfinding peers want you to admit that you made a bad judgment call. You may not agree and, without sugarcoating it, that's a difficult pill to swallow. As a result, feelings are hurt on both sides, team morale is seriously injured, and productivity is sidetracked.

For your own protection, stand up for yourself. But do try to make friends with your critics before they attempt to damage your other relationships, such as with your boss, for instance.

SQUAWKERS

Squawkers are chronic gripers who grumble about everything—publicly and secretly.

It's their cruel and harsh manner of correcting you that sets your teeth on edge. For a minor infraction, they'll ridicule you before the entire staff or send an email blast to the entire team. Besides grumbling about you, their firing away at other colleagues leaves you wondering how to respond.

Even more destructive is the way they wrap complaints in "confidential" information and then tie you up by swearing you to secrecy. Instead of knocking out the problem with a frank talk right to the heart of the matter, you're left boxing with shadows.

What You're Thinking

According to Eleanor, Lincoln is about to stick a knife in my back because he thinks his team should be handling every aspect of orientation instead of my team. Her information source swore her to secrecy, so Eleanor says if I say anything to Lincoln, she'll deny telling me and his folks will be in hot water. Eleanor claims she told me this so that I could defend myself. How can I ward off an attack when I don't have all the information and I can't talk to the alleged perpetrator?

A Squawker's Thoughts

Eve and Lincoln cut me out of the orientation altogether. They completely overlooked my training experience and the good suggestions I could offer them. Well, I don't think they'll be trusting each other so much anymore. And the irony is that Eve will now feel she owes me one for tipping her off! Once the two of them start squabbling, I can let the boss know I'm available to handle the project.

When being attacked, your first goal is to minimize damage, and the second is to try to convert your enemy into a friend.

1. *Do a quick review.* Race over the facts leading up to this point. Did you inadvertently trigger the trouble? Have you assumed colleague support without bothering to check?

2. *Don't play their I've-got-a-secret game.* Refuse to promise to keep confidential your peer's gossip or rumor. Get the issue on the table so that you can deal with it.

3. *Dissolve the tension by talking.* You can't let cutting remarks fester. Politely confront your accuser. Then examine the system that allowed the problem to arise. Discuss options. If a colleague unfairly criticized you at a staff meeting, meet later in private to hash it out.

4. *Touch base regularly with potential troublemakers.* Keep your peers informed about your projects. Involve them by coordinating appropriate segments. Before they squawk to the boss about you, listen to, understand, and be cooperative about their complaints. Suggest joint presentations with the modifications you agree on. And give them the starring roles.

5. *Insist on respect for yourself and your peers.* Simply refuse to continue a conversation unless everyone is civil. If a peer complains about another colleague to you, you can't escape by keeping still. To a Squawker, *remaining silent means you agree.* If you think the third party is indeed causing a problem, decide how you

are going to deal with it. If you disagree, speak up and say why you feel as you do.

TACTICAL TALK

You: *I'm sorry, Eleanor, but if I keep your secret, I can't solve the problem. I am going to talk to Lincoln without mentioning any names. I know you don't realize it, Eleanor, but somebody is using you to stir up trouble. You don't want to be involved in that, do you?*

Or: *Lincoln, I heard you were concerned that your team is not handling the entire orientation. We've always worked well together. I'm sure you have some good ideas for straightening this out.*

Or: *I can understand why you were upset, Lincoln. Why don't we figure out the best approach and go together to the boss? You tell him what we agreed on, and I'll back you up.*

Or: *I really don't want to argue about this. I'll come back when we can talk calmly.*

Or: *What you say about Joseph may be true, but my experience with him has been just the opposite. I've found him to be totally dependable. For example, when I was handling the spring conference . . .*

Or: *Hold on a minute, Eleanor. You haven't stopped griping for the past fifteen minutes. Why don't we give it a rest and talk only about pleasant things for the remainder of our lunch hour, okay?*

> **Tip:** The trouble with Squawkers is that they do too much squawking and you don't do enough talking. When you're attacked, confront your accusers and resolve the matter. Early consulting and coordinating with them on a regular basis usually takes the sting out of their bite.

SUPERSENSITIVES

Supersensitives are extremely touchy and take every comment as a personal affront.

What your colleagues do in their private lives is their own business, until it affects you. Then you have to talk about your mutual concern. But the Supersensitives get tense, touchy, and uptight. Without your criticizing them, they act defensively. No matter what you say, it's suddenly you against them.

Why the irrational reaction to imagined criticism? Supersensitives lack confidence in themselves or feel inferior to you, and they are hurt much too easily. You and your colleagues, having lost patience with their immature behavior, avoid them like the plague, and they don't know why.

But now you have to talk.

What You're Thinking

All I said to Serenity was that I wanted to talk to her about the delay in routing top-priority items. She instantly jumped down my throat for my claiming the delay was her fault. She began reciting her virtues—she's the first one to show up for work, she puts in more hours than I do, she's not lazy like some other managers, and on and on. We never did discuss the routing problem.

A Supersensitive's Thoughts

When Carlos came by to talk about the delay, I could see what he was up to. He was about to criticize the way I run my division and imply that I'm not as efficient as he is. Well, I resent his superior attitude. I guess I put him down a peg or two.

STRATEGY

Your goal is to overcome or at least tone down the Supersensitives' resentment. You want to resolve a difficulty or deliver negative feedback without getting into an extended argument. When you're having trouble talking to Supersensitives, the tactics in this checklist will help.

CHECKLIST FOR DEALING WITH SUPERSENSITIVES

❏ Do I help build their self-confidence? Ask them to review your work and suggest changes. Your gratitude will raise their own self-respect.

❏ Do I help them balance their feelings? Do you get them to express their hurt directly and honestly? If you contributed to their hurt feelings, apologize. If their feelings appear irrational, ask them to look again at the facts.

❏ Do I protect their pride? They feel humiliated if you discuss a problem in front of others. Keep it private.

❏ Have I acknowledged their needs? Recognize their requirements without assuming blame or guilt. Simply add what you, too, need—and why.

❏ Do I soften the sting? Wedge a criticism between two compliments. Talk as teammates working together. Say, "We did," rather than "You did."

❏ Do I let the boss handle their poor performance? If they don't do their jobs right, that's the boss's responsibility, not yours. When you poke your nose into somebody else's turf, they have a right to resent it.

❏ Do I skip lengthy prologues? Get right to the point. Otherwise they sense something is coming. Your stalling makes them anxious and exaggerates the importance of the discussion.

❏ Do I state issues factually? Be prepared with specific names, numbers, places, dates, and frequency. Use questions to expose underlying problems.

❏ Do I keep the discussion substantive? After you acknowledge their feelings, stick to the facts, objectives, obstacles, and tactics. Skip the talk about attitudes, motives, or who's to blame.

❏ Have we agreed on a plan? Develop specific stages or tasks to get from here to there. If the steps are complicated, remain upbeat as you both develop an outline. Email the plan to create a paper trail and to ensure accountability.

TACTICAL TALK

You: *Serenity, would you mind taking a look at this chart I've designed? Do you see any steps I might be able to eliminate?*

Or: *Please tell me frankly what it was I did or said that seems to have hurt your feelings.*

Or: *I understand that you need . . . But I have a tight schedule that requires . . . Really, I'm not trying to put you down; I just want to do my job a little better.*

Or: *We run into this snag about three times a week. How can we realistically circumvent the roadblock? . . . Then why don't we work up a new schedule?*

Tip: Reduce the resentment of Supersensitives by helping them deal honestly with their feelings. Usually, they have been isolated because of their foolish behavior. They need to regain their self-respect and know they're capable of contributing. They have to distinguish between imagined slurs and real facts. You can make a big difference by becoming friends with these critics.

WISECRACKERS

Wisecrackers toss witty and sarcastic jokes about your flaws.

With Supersensitives, it's obvious they're upset. With Wisecrackers, you're left guessing. These colleagues are quick with quips and put-downs that disguise their antagonism. They know your shortcomings and may suspect you created the error, but they don't come right out and say so. Their nonassertiveness leaves you confused.

Wisecrackers enjoy subtle and indirect jabs, especially with an audience to appreciate their wit and protect them. You may be facing a very difficult situation, yet they feel free to criticize because they carry no responsibility toward you or your feelings. The buried, unresolved conflict leaves your alliance on shaky ground.

What You're Thinking

When Kayden made that crack about my putting all those business lunches on the tab, he wasn't just joking. He meant to insult me. How can I laugh at his remarks and keep overlooking the fact that he's holding me up to ridicule? Even if I did goof, there's no way I could have responded without losing face. I've got to find a way to stop him from repeatedly embarrassing me in front of the team.

A Wisecracker's Thoughts

Why should Ryder get away with those long, expensive lunches? I resent the boss always asking him to talk to the prospective clients when I can certainly represent the company as well as or better than Ryder. My little jokes will let Ryder know I've got my eye on him.

Your goal is to minimize the effect of the Wisecrackers' remarks and, if possible, to curb their resentment or hostility.

1. *Own up to a mistake.* If your error is exposed to a group, admit, apologize, and briefly explain. Assume your explanation will be accepted. If you expound, point by point, it looks like you expect them to find you guilty—and they most likely will.

2. *Make light of a public "attack."* Without becoming defensive, move the subject away from yourself and talk policy or procedure. If the disguised jokes continue, seek peer support by asking if the others agree. Start teasing the Wisecrackers yourself. Their other victims in the group will probably be happy to join you.

3. *Practice at home to take the offensive.* Hearing how you sound on video will help you develop a confident and conversational tone. By role-playing with a friend, you can practice making direct eye contact as well as adopting a sincere and relaxed manner. Critique your performance by reviewing the recording. Keep practicing until you are more comfortable.

4. *In private, bring hostility to the surface.* Wisecrackers will claim they were only teasing, but they persist in digging. Unemotionally, tell them how you felt. Ask the Wisecrackers to be up-front with you, then deal with the real problem.

5. *Disarm your attackers.* Keep your colleagues informed. Give them a chance to buy into your project or proposal. Get them to express to you their thinking, suggestions, and disagreements in the early stages, rather than springing the finished product on the group and inviting the wisecracks.

You: *Kayden, something you said yesterday really bothered me, and I'd like to settle it.*

Or: *Maybe to you it was just teasing, but to me it felt like I was run over by an avalanche.*

Or: *Kayden, it really would help us both if you'd level with me and tell me what's really bothering you, so we could clear it up.*

> **Tip:** Wisecrackers go far beyond friendly teasing during their public performances. Malicious intent lurks behind their brand of humor. Instead of becoming defensive, change the channel and talk about what's wrong with the system. Then take the offensive and start teasing the teasers. Later, in private, deal openly with their hostility.

WET BLANKETS

Wet Blankets quickly douse the flames whenever colleagues are fired up with enthusiasm or creativity.

While most of us concur that constructive criticism is essential in evaluating an idea, Wet Blankets don't want to go through that process. Without examining the factors, they've already decided, "It won't work!"

Too often, this declaration stops discussion dead in its tracks. It takes only a few negativists to smother a healthy workplace environment. When monkey wrenches are constantly thrown into the momentum, some talented workers don't feel like fighting the effect of them, and they leave. Others are discouraged and slow down the good pace of their work.

How do you counteract a Wet Blanket's conviction that, if you proceed, the sky will fall and there's nothing you can do to stop it? They feel—and make you feel—that the situation is beyond your control. But you don't have to accept *their* reality.

What You're Thinking

I thought it was a good idea to approach the boss about rotating our schedules. That would give each of us a week of four days working in the office and one day working remotely. I think the others might have gone along with me. Then Brad chimes in, as usual. He sure knows how to rip any proposal apart, which is okay, but he offers no help in making it better. Just drop it because it can't work, he says. A few generalities from him and the mood changed. It was like air fizzling out of a balloon.

A Wet Blanket's Thoughts

It's a good thing I was there to head them off such a crazy idea. They know the boss would never agree to something like that. He wants instant contact with all of us. He won't trust us to do any work he can't directly supervise. A few years back he turned down my request to do a special project at home. I tried it before—it didn't work then, and it won't work now.

STRATEGY

Your goal is to reduce the Wet Blankets' pessimistic influence, clearing the way for realistic planning.

1. *Construct support before offering your plan.* Save your conclusion until the group has examined the various elements. When possible, point to relevant similar ideas that have worked successfully in the past.

2. *Acknowledge that problem areas exist.* You can't change the personalities of Wet Blankets, but this will allow you to alter the outcome. Instead of arguing, admit that perhaps your original thinking should be modified, and ask for their specific objections. Also, ask Wet Blankets what would be the worst-case scenario if you go ahead with this idea.

3. *Keep control of the discussion.* Wet Blankets have a habit of interrupting to interject their doom and gloom. Don't let them. Interrupt the interrupter and keep going.

4. *Sincerely suggest ways to help Wet Blankets with their careers.* Make them aware of how negativity can hold them back. Explain the importance of being fair and listening without interrupting to the entire proposal before handing it a death sentence.

TACTICAL TALK

Brad: *There are all kinds of holes in this idea. The boss will never let us do it.*

You: *Sure, Brad, this presents some red flags. Let's take a closer look at what we can do before deciding on any definite procedure. What is it, specifically, that bothers you? What's the worst that can happen if we go ahead with it?*

Brad: *We know it won't work, so why invite tighter scrutiny from the boss? Remember a few years ago when I told the boss I could finish the Whiting project faster without interruptions and traveling time if I could do it at home? No, he's got to see us working to believe that we are.*

You: *This really isn't the same as the situation you're remembering. For one thing, now we all have smartphones and remote access, so he can reach us instantly. It seems to me that there's more of a comparison with the time last year when Katie broke her leg and she* was able to send in her reports, working from home on her laptop. Anyway, as I was saying, the plan would have to—

Brad: *(Interrupting.)* You're just spinning your wheels. There's no way this can be approved when the boss—

You: *(Interrupting.)* Pardon me, Brad, just let me finish this point, and then we can take up any special difficulties you foresee. I think the idea is worth a try. How about the rest of you? Are you with me?

Or:

You: *(Private discussion.)* Brad, I know how much you care about our team and that you're trying to protect us. However, I don't think you realize the effect of what you do. By spreading that not-a-hope-in-hell feeling each time an idea is proposed, you make others regard you as a pessimist. This could hold you back because people won't want to work with you, and bosses look for workers who are positive and capable of developing new ideas. Would you mind if I give you a few tips that I've learned over the years?

> **Tip:** Avoid being hoodwinked into believing there are no viable alternatives. Just because Wet Blankets say so doesn't mean you have to accept their doom. With careful examination and planning, you can minimize potential problems and stress the benefits of trying.

When colleagues find fault, you can accept the fact that someone disagrees with you without accepting the criticism itself. If you agree that you *are* at fault, immediately apologize and suggest a remedy. But when you consider the remark to be unfair, you can say we all have a right to our opinions and present your point.

Don't let yourself be pulled under by Rumormongers who swear you to secrecy, or the overly sensitive who fight unnecessary battles, or joking colleagues who mask their jabs, or peers who spread doom and gloom. Admittedly, their acts aren't amicable, but it's in *your* best interest to remain friendly and foster good team spirit.

CHAPTER 30

WHEN YOUR SUBORDINATES ARE FAULTFINDERS

- **Blame Shifters**
- **Whiners**
- **Self-Beraters**
- **Martyrs**

If your subordinates are constantly complaining, the feedback line is probably clogged. You especially need an ongoing, flowing communication system that connects the thinking between you and your workers when dealing with faultfinding subordinates who charge you with their errors, snitch on their colleagues, or blame themselves for every mistake.

It's easy to second-guess others, so don't assume sinister motives. The worker who appears to be goofing off might see himself as conscientiously laboring even though he's ill. The assistant who is dissing you never once told you that she feels overburdened. You don't know what people are thinking unless they tell you, and the best way to find out is to ask.

Such dialogue moves you toward the mutual goal of transparency and improved performance. Most people want to do better and, as their boss, you want them to, also. Learn to capitalize on their criticism by using it as a springboard for discussion.

BLAME SHIFTERS

Blame Shifters blame you for their own boneheaded blunders.

They are buck-passers. Once they report a serious problem to you, it's your migraine. They've washed their hands of any further responsibility. When the anticipated disaster occurs, they have already transferred the mistake to you, their scapegoat. It's all your fault.

Blame Shifters have difficulty handling pressure. If they feel you're criticizing them, they have to relieve their hurt or fear or worry. So they remove the blame from themselves and hand it to you. You don't help them develop by promising to think about a matter they bring to you; that just saddles you with more worries about assignments that should have remained delegated.

What You're Thinking

Tina should have had all the data for the application together by now. She said she informed me a few weeks ago that she was having trouble finding the information. She claims I told her I'd get back to her about it. I probably did say that, but with so much on my mind, wouldn't you think she'd check back with me? Now we don't have enough time to do a thorough job. I'm angry that I couldn't depend on Tina, while she acts as though I am totally responsible for blowing this opportunity.

A Blame Shifter's Thoughts

I was worried about making the deadline, so I told the boss I was having trouble finding the information for the application. He was supposed to give me some direction, and I'm still waiting for him to "get back" to me. Now he's blaming me for not following through with my assignment.

You can't win in this job. Bosses always have to have someone to blame for their mistakes, and the criticism flows in only one direction—down.

STRATEGY

Your goal is to get the Blame Shifters to accept responsibility for their own behavior. Start by reducing the emotional overload.

1. *Let them voice their anger or frustration.* Be empathetic, anxious to know what they think. Listen, without responding to the charges. Blame Shifters will try to make you their victims. Even if you contributed to a misunderstanding, that doesn't relieve them of their obligations.

2. *Suggest that you meet soon.* You both need a little time to compose yourselves. Should the Blame Shifters' complaints be legitimate, you'll want to correct your action. When the atmosphere is calm again, start resolving the difficulty.

3. *Define the real problem.* Start by complimenting Blame Shifters on specific matters they handled well. Then point out the trouble spots. Keep the discussion impersonal.

4. *Don't do your subordinates' work for them.* Make them responsible for working on the solution and following through. Explain the consequences they face if they don't produce. Ask them to specify the tasks that have to be done and to set reasonable deadlines. Have them send you a recap email to make sure you're on the same page. Now, let go! There's a plan and a date; forget about the matter until then.

TACTICAL TALK

You: *Tina, maybe I didn't make myself clear. . . . But now we have a serious matter we have to deal with. I think we both need a little while to sort our thoughts. Please be back here at 3 PM.*

Or: *Tina, I appreciate the amount of work you've been handling, but I'm not pleased when I depend on staff to come through and then learn something's not done. What do you suggest we do about this?*

Or: *Now that we have some ideas for changing procedures, what would you need to salvage the application? What kind of help do you need?*

Or: *Okay, if I assign Katie and Tim to help you, you understand you have full responsibility for getting it done on time and you are aware of what will happen if you miss the deadline. Email me on Friday to tell me how you're progressing.*

> **Tip:** Foil Blame Shifters who try to victimize you by handing you their mistakes and responsibilities. Don't contribute to their antics by promising to give them an answer later on. Help them by discussing the problem, and let them suggest ways to handle it. Then stay on top of the matter through clearly defined reporting procedures.

WHINERS

Whiners are crybabies who voice protracted protests over the unimportant.

Driven by childish insecurity, Whiners complain when everything's actually going well. They love to exaggerate unfair workloads, tardy reports, broken rules—whatever they can blame on somebody else. Although their work is good, they're interested only in their own success. They cause dissension and destroy morale by tattling on their colleagues.

Occasionally, they hit on a problem with roots in the system, and this has to be hashed over and remedied. But usually Whiners don't sound off about legitimate problems. Yet they can be so persuasive, you end up defending yourself and feeling foolish later. When Whiners warn you of trouble ahead, their intent is to establish an excuse in advance of a feared failure. If the complaint involves their peers, they want you to referee and decide in their favor.

What You're Thinking

I can hardly believe it. With all the critical decisions that are weighing me down, Denise parades in here complaining that Alice is playing her music too loudly and that it is making everyone else uncomfortable. When I told her that was between her and Alice, she said Alice insulted her and they got into a fight. Now she wants me to referee. How did I get into this? And more important, how do I get out?

A Whiner's Thoughts

I told Alice that playing her music so loudly was a very selfish thing to do and that she only cares about herself. She has no consideration for anybody else. I warned her that if she didn't stop acting like that, I would report her. I'm glad I did. It's bad enough that I don't get the recognition I deserve around here, without having to suffer from headaches as well.

STRATEGY

Your goal is to improve team morale by helping the Whiners act in a more mature and professional manner.

1. *Reassure the Whiners.* They may be using petty complaints to get you to say something nice to them. Try more frequent feedback to recognize their accomplishments, allay their fears or insecurities,

and offer your support. Keep checking to learn if things are okay before they hatch minor matters into full-scale complaints.

2. *Lead them toward more appropriate behavior.* Ask them how they feel after acting in certain (inappropriate) ways and what part their behavior had in bringing about the result. You can be empathetic and noncritical and still help Whiners realize that they were part of the problem and should be part of the solution.

3. *Refuse to be the referee.* Don't take sides, either in petty bickering or if the squabble blows up and the whole office is abuzz. When it gets that bad, you have to step in, but get the facts before you do. Don't blame anyone or let them rehash accusations. To restore teamwork, get them to recognize that they both have individual needs, and that they both must focus on how these needs can be met.

4. *Distinguish between a Whiner's exaggerated cry and a common complaint.* If you're concerned that the criticism may be more widespread than you first realized, use your staff meetings to resolve the problem. Give the group an exercise in finding solutions.

TACTICAL TALK

You: *Denise, I'd like you to set aside from 9 to 9:15 every Thursday morning to meet with me. I'm starting a separate "How's it going?" time with each of my staff, so be prepared to talk about any problems or ideas you want to bring to my attention.*

Or: *Denise, I understand you're upset. I, too, find it disturbing that you couldn't work out the problem with Alice. What result were you hoping for? . . . How did you feel after you told Alice to stop? . . . Do you think the way you asked may have brought on her reaction? . . . What options are open now to get what you want?*

Or: *I've called you both in here because the present situation cannot continue. It's affecting the entire office. I want the problem resolved; how* *about you? We all know what led up to this point, so let's not review it. Let's define what we want to accomplish. Well, what are your needs? . . . How could that be prevented? . . . You've made a good start. You don't need me anymore to work out a tentative answer. Tell me on Friday what the two of you have come up with.*

Tip: The Whiners' bids for attention are juvenile, but their need to be noticed is real. To bolster their sense of security, help them focus on objectives and learn how to get along instead of being a tattletale on their peers. Don't fall into their trap by playing referee. If you do, as soon as one complaint is resolved, Whiners will be ready with another.

SELF-BERATERS

Self-Beraters nag themselves and believe that whatever went wrong was their fault.

Like Whiners, they are looking for reassurance. But instead of picking on their peers, they peck at themselves. They are overly critical of their own work. They dramatize how bad they're doing so that you'll contradict them. They claim blame for whatever went amiss, hoping you'll grant them absolution. Actually, they perform well, but they are so insecure that they have to plead for compliments.

Having such low self-esteem, Self-Beraters are always anxious and practically invite people to take advantage of them. Their way to avoid being hurt by others is to inflict the hurt on themselves before anyone else can do it to them. You find it difficult to criticize them because they've already attacked themselves more severely than you ever would.

What You're Thinking

Just to stop the emotional blackmail, I find myself tempted to give in to Darren's begging for compliments. Sometimes I think it would be less nerve-racking to assure him, over and over and over, "Yes, you're doing a great job." It's as though he's bracing himself to be hurt or scolded. Instead, when I do compliment Darren, he can't accept it graciously. His demand for reassurance is insatiable.

A Self-Berater's Thoughts

That report I gave the boss probably wasn't any good, or I would have heard from her by now. I guess after being knocked down as many times as I have, I have to conclude that I can't do anything right. I think maybe the boss is avoiding me. What else did I do wrong? I'm such an ignoramus. I should have spent more time on that report. It's all my fault that the boss doesn't like it.

STRATEGY

Your goal is to salvage good workers by helping Self-Beraters become more emotionally mature. Once they gain confidence, they'll stop the annoying habit of putting themselves down.

1. *Continue giving them assignments they do well.* Offer help if they need it, and leave them alone if they don't. Allow them to experience a lot of little successes to feel more secure and bolster their self-confidence in the good work they are capable of performing.
2. *Get them to talk about their concerns.* Once they can discuss what's making them feel anxious and look at it for what it is, they can deal with it. But as long as they cover up their fears with

self-incrimination, they'll keep deprecating themselves to counteract anticipated criticism.

3. *Explain the cost of begging for reassurance.* Recognize good work, but don't reinforce their habit by pumping out reassurance upon request. Make clear the negative effect this has on others.

TACTICAL TALK

Darren: *I guess my report was pretty bad.*

You: *Darren, wait until you've goofed up as many times as I have before you start putting yourself down. Actually, the report was sharp and incisive.*

Darren: *You're just saying that to be nice. You don't really mean it, do you?*

You: *I don't say things I don't mean, and I find it upsetting when someone doubts my word. On Tuesday, I'd like you to present to my management committee excerpts that you can highlight.*

Darren: *You really want me to do that? I don't know if I can—*

You: *(Interrupting.) I know you can, so suppose you tell me what you're really concerned about.*

Or: *I'm glad we had this talk, Darren. If you wait to be propped up by constant reassurance, you'll lose out on many good opportunities. But you decide, and let me know tomorrow.*

Tip: Don't baby the Self-Beraters by spoon-feeding them compliments upon demand. You stunt their growth if you pay their emotional blackmail. When they cry for reassurance, give them the jobs they can handle and the recognition they deserve. Do what's reasonable to help them build self-confidence, and get them to identify and deal with their real concerns.

MARTYRS

Martyrs complain about how much they've sacrificed when you never even asked for their help.

These workhorses create resentment because they gripe about being overworked but won't accept help. They email you in the middle of the night to make sure you know that they worked late, even though you didn't ask them to do so. They want you to feel dependent upon them. If they accept the offers of assistance, other workers might pick up their skills and the Martyrs might find themselves out in the cold.

They are obsessive workaholics who use work to smother some personal problem. When they fail, the fault is never theirs. Martyrs are indeed exploited because they volunteer their slave labor. While they complain about unfair distribution of assignments, they really enjoy their suffering as they watch others fail to meet their exhaustingly high level of performance.

What You're Thinking

Leo doesn't fool anyone but himself. He insists on taking the hardest cases. Then they pile up and he won't accept a lift with the load. It's pretty obvious to me that he resents his peers because he's doing some of their work. Although he tries to suppress the resentment, they see it also. And, because he refuses their help, they feel angry instead of grateful to him. Leo's frantic pace and antagonistic attitude are making everyone else tense. How can I stop this merry-go-round?

A Martyr's Thoughts

They are all a bunch of ingrates. I stay late every night to clean up the worst cases, and they don't appreciate what I'm doing for them. Don't they know if I didn't do it, it wouldn't get done? At least, it wouldn't get done as well. Yet nobody cares how great my work is. I don't get the right recognition from the boss or anyone else. But I'll be the good little team player and not say anything.

STRATEGY

Your goal is to stop unnecessary tension by resolving a legitimate criticism—an imbalance in the workload. If you control the Martyrs, everyone can resume working at a reasonable rate.

1. *Produce a plan to redistribute the work.* When Martyrs protect their workload like mother hens, scratching everyone else in the process, it's time to change the mix. Giving each worker new assignments will prevent overburdening. It also loosens the Martyrs' grip and dispels the reason for resentment.

2. *Politely refuse excessive help.* Within seconds, the compulsive Martyrs will again be volunteering. Don't accept. Keep their assignments within the limits you set. Martyrs have a personal problem, and they'll have to find some way to deal with it other than driving everybody in the office crazy.

3. *Be more generous with recognition.* Utilize the talents of the Martyrs by recognizing their excellence and persuading them to help you coach others.

TACTICAL TALK

You: *We're making some needed changes around here so that there's a more equitable workload. This new assignment sheet . . .*

Or: *Thanks, Leo. I appreciate your wanting to take on more work, but I have something more important for you to do. You'll notice that you're* *down for a planning session with me. I want you to head a new unit because I need your special expertise to help me train . . .*

> **Tip:** Hold fast to limiting the amount of work you let the Martyrs do. Give them more recognition for their dedicated performance. This won't make them less compulsive, but it should produce a happier atmosphere in your office. Subordinate griping is good when it forces you to stop going around in circles and start moving forward toward improved performance. Help your workers develop by empowering them to be responsible for their own actions. Show them how to convert their anger into new energy and new answers.

Sometimes you need private conversations to uncover the source of frustration, and talking it through points out the way to go. However, if clashes emanate from poor rules or directives, you can utilize team huddles, staff meetings, and other brainstorming sessions to throw some problems back at your people. Then consider their recommendations. Talking to each other—listening and responding—and finally resolving the criticism leads to increased loyalty and productivity.

SUMMING IT UP

- **26 Tactful Phrases to Help You Confront Difficult People**
- **10 Important Guidelines to Remember**

26 TACTFUL PHRASES TO HELP YOU CONFRONT DIFFICULT PEOPLE

When you know you should confront, you tend to either lash out or back off. You either become the attack dog or suffer silently. The trick is to keep your words impersonal. Here are useful openers for getting your point across while maintaining professional dignity.

WHEN YOU DISAGREE:

- ❏ It seems to me that the problem is . . .
- ❏ My concern is that we may not have enough . . .
- ❏ Please explain this to me. There appears to be an error. . . .
- ❏ While I don't agree with your conclusion, you certainly have the right to your opinion.
- ❏ Would it be possible for you to recheck . . . ?

WHEN YOU'RE INTERRUPTED:

❏ Pardon me, I'm not through. Just give me a few seconds to finish my point.

WHEN YOU RUN INTO A BUZZ SAW:

❏ Obviously, you're too upset to discuss this now. I'll talk to you later.
❏ We don't have to agree, but is there any reason we can't be civil to each other?
❏ I can see why you may feel that way. . . .
❏ You'd have every right to feel that way if that were the case.
❏ I understand you have a problem with that, but I expect to be treated with courtesy, respect, and the professionalism I've earned.
❏ Please tell me frankly what I've done to offend you.

WHEN YOU'RE BEING PRESSURED:

❏ I don't feel totally comfortable [with that] [talking about that]. . . .
❏ Don't you think it would be a good idea to hold off until . . . ?

WHEN YOU REPRIMAND:

❏ What steps would you suggest to correct that?
❏ I'm sure you don't realize it, but . . .
❏ Perhaps you didn't understand the consequences that could result from . . .
❏ Maybe I failed to make myself clear. . . .

WHEN YOU WANT TO EXPRESS YOUR ANGER:

❏ I have to tell you that I felt offended by that remark.

❏ I was upset when I realized the decision was based on . . .

❏ I felt I was treated badly when I wasn't informed in advance about
the change.

WHEN YOU WANT TO CLEAR UP CONFUSION:

❏ I'd appreciate your help with this muddled negotiation. Is it true
that you said . . . ?

❏ When all the facts are in and verified, it will be apparent that . . .

❏ It looks like following this system got our signals crossed. However,
we can . . .

❏ Perhaps I misunderstood. Are you saying that . . . ?

❏ Let me see if I understand this. Would I be correct in assuming that
you feel . . . ?

10 IMPORTANT GUIDELINES TO REMEMBER

How you deal with a specific boss, colleague, or subordinate who's cur-
rently making your life miserable depends on the outcome you want to
accomplish. However, several general guidelines can help you.

1. *Put problem people in proper perspective.* You're nothing but an
    afterthought to them, so don't take their antics personally. They're
    not concerned about you because they're too busy worrying about
    themselves. You just happen to be either an obstacle or an essential
    ingredient to their getting what they want. You have to figure out
    how to break free of their control.

2. *Take your pick—positive or negative.* You can't concentrate on constructive, creative alternatives while you cling to negative feelings. Go somewhere to vent your emotions and cool off. Think about the result you really want, the consequence or outcome that most benefits you. That will help you let go of the hurt.

3. *Don't expect difficult people to change.* They won't—and in one way that's good. Because their behavior is often predictable, this enables you to plan ahead, plotting the tactics you'll use the next time. Troublemakers may not change, but by choosing a better approach, you can change the outcome.

4. *Learn to respond as well as to listen.* Come forward and state that you feel annoyed, upset, enraged. No one can read your mind. Sometimes the offense was totally unintentional and can be easily resolved if allowed to surface. Ask questions instead of making accusations. If you let others save face, you give them room to change their minds.

5. *Give and request frequent feedback.* Regardless of your position in the organization, you need to know the perceptions of your boss, peers, and workers. Don't stew about what someone else may be thinking—ask! Use open-ended questions to let emotional people vent their feelings before you try to reason with them and explore options. When you link your objectives with another's wants, not only do you have his or her attention, but you both win something.

6. *Look at policies and procedures first.* That starts the discussion on a professional level and prevents blaming a person's distasteful attitude or sinister motive. Don't place blame unless *you* made a mistake for which you apologize quickly and move on. If you both pay attention to each other's needs when identifying

options—your stand may depend on which side of the desk you sit on—each of you can feel you are exercising some control. At times all that's needed is a simple change in the system.

7. *Deal directly and discreetly.* You don't want an audience for personal disagreements. Confront your accusers, tactfully putting your foot down when others are walking all over you. Get right to the point; a preamble of excuses or warm-ups robs your effectiveness. Choose face-to-face talks or phone calls over emails or text messages. After all, tone and inflection can be easily misconstrued in a written message. Still, it is a great tactic to follow up an oral dialogue with an emailed recap.

8. *Document for self-protection.* Get potentially troublesome verbal agreements in writing to prevent the other party from reneging. On assignments you fear may be hazardous to the health of your career, keep your boss informed with periodic progress reports. Copy all relevant parties on emails, as evidence, in case a misunderstanding should occur. Create a separate Outlook folder, so that you may easily store and retrieve these messages for which you've created a "paper trail."

9. *Be straightforward and unemotional.* The more you remain calm and matter-of-fact, the sooner you gain another's confidence. People want to feel you're leveling with them, that they can trust you. Remember that respect from others begins with self-respect. Don't continue a conversation with anyone, even your boss, who refuses to give you the courtesy you deserve. You have options, such as asking for politeness or leaving the room.

10. *Be gracious.* Someone else's rudeness doesn't give you the right to be rude. Turn a bad situation to your advantage by disarming the offenders, treating them with the kindness you'd like to be shown,

sharing credit, and allowing others to feel important. Make friends with your enemies—you never know when you'll need them. Others won't have to run you down to build themselves up if you're gracious in showing appreciation and giving recognition. When your own ego is healthy, you are rich. You can afford to be generous.

ABOUT THE AUTHORS

Amy Cooper Hakim is an industrial-organizational psychology practitioner. She holds a Ph.D. in the field and is the principal consultant at the Cooper Strategic Group. She helps employees and employers to get along better and coaches leaders and employees to improve productivity, morale, satisfaction, and overall work-life balance. Dr. Hakim also has more than twelve years of online teaching experience in business, management, leadership, and psychology courses. She and her husband, Elad, reside in South Florida and are the proud parents of three children. For consulting or speaking arrangements, please contact her at amycooperhakim.com.

Muriel Solomon was a business communication consultant with forty years professional experience. Her syndicated column on managing conflict within organizations began in the *Miami Herald* and appeared for many years throughout the United States, Canada, and Europe. Through national periodicals, lectures, and media appearances, she taught companies her own "Strategic Talking" method for getting desired results. Ms. Solomon was the author of *"What Do I Say When . . ."*: *A Guidebook for Getting Your Way with People on the Job, Getting Praised, Raised and Recognized*, and *Getting What You Want and Deserve*. She passed away in 2004, surrounded by family and loved ones.

INDEX